Criminalized Lives

Q+ Public

Andrew Spieldenner, Cal State University San Marcos; MPact: Global Action for Gay Health & Rights; United States People Living with HIV Caucus

The Q+ Public books are a limited series of curated volumes, based on the seminal journal *OUT/LOOK: National Lesbian and Gay Quarterly*. *OUT/LOOK* was a political and cultural quarterly published out of San Francisco from 1988 to 1992. It was the first new publication to bring together lesbians and gay men after a decade or more of political and cultural separatism. It was consciously multigender and racially inclusive, addressed politics and culture, wrested with controversial topics, and emphasized visual material along with scholarly and creative writing. *OUT/LOOK* built a bridge between academic inquiry and the broader community. Q+ Public promises to revive *OUT/LOOK*'s political and cultural agenda in a new format, and revitalize a queer public sphere to bring together academics, intellectuals, and artists to explore questions that urgently concern all LGBTQ+ communities.

For a complete list of titles in the series, please see the last page of the book.

Criminalized Lives

~

HIV and Legal Violence

ALEXANDER McCLELLAND

ILLUSTRATIONS BY ERIC KOSTIUK WILLIAMS

Rutgers University Press

New Brunswick, Camden, and Newark, New Jersey

London and Oxford

Rutgers University Press is a department of Rutgers, The State University of New Jersey, one of the leading public research universities in the nation. By publishing worldwide, it furthers the University's mission of dedication to excellence in teaching, scholarship, research, and clinical care.

Library of Congress Cataloging-in-Publication Data

Names: McClelland, Alexander, author. | Williams, Eric Kostiuk, illustrator.
Title: Criminalized lives: HIV & legal violence / Alexander McClelland;
illustrations by Eric Kostiuk Williams.
Description: New Brunswick: Rutgers University Press, 2024. | Series:
Q+ public | Includes bibliographical references and index.
Identifiers: LCCN 2023047786 | ISBN 9781978832053 (paperback) |
ISBN 9781978832060 (hardcover) | ISBN 9781978832077 (epub) |
ISBN 9781978832091 (pdf)
Subjects: LCSH: HIV infections—Law and legislation—Canada—
Criminal provisions. | Sexually transmitted diseases—Law
and legislation—Canada—Criminal provisions. | HIV-positive
persons—Legal status, laws, etc.—Canada. | AIDS (Disease)—
Transmission—Canada. | Liability (Law)—Canada. |
Violence (Law)—Canada.
Classification: LCC KE3593.A54 M33 2024 | DDC 345.71/0242—
dc23/eng/20240126
LC record available at https://lccn.loc.gov/2023047786

A British Cataloging-in-Publication record for this book is available from
the British Library.

∞ The paper used in this publication meets the requirements of the American
National Standard for Information Sciences—Permanence of Paper for
Printed Library Materials, ANSI Z39.48-1992.

rutgersuniversitypress.org

This book is dedicated to J., C., M., J., S., and M.

What does it mean to protest suffering, as distinct from acknowledging it?
—Susan Sontag, *Regarding the Pain of Others*

What does it mean to live in a negative relation to the law?
—Colin Dayan, *The Law Is a White Dog: How Legal Rituals Make and Unmake Persons*

Contents

Illustrations

Series Introduction

Q+ Public is a series of small thematic books in which leading scholars, artists, community leaders, activists, independent writers, and thinkers engage in critical reflection on contemporary LGBTQ+ political, social, and cultural issues.

Q+ Public is about elevating the challenges of thinking about gender, sex, and sexuality across complex and diverse identities to offer a forum for public dialogue.

Q+ Public is an outgrowth, after a long hibernation, of *OUT/LOOK Lesbian and Gay Quarterly*, a pioneering political and cultural journal that sparked intense national debate over the five years it was published, 1988 to 1992. As an early (and incomplete) model of intersectional inclusion, *OUT/LOOK* was the first publication since the early 1970s to bring together lesbians and gay men after years of separate movements. The visual and written content of *OUT/LOOK* addressed complex gender roles (with a blind spot about transgender issues), was racially diverse, embraced political and cultural topics that were controversial or had not yet been articulated, and emphasized visual art along with scholarly and creative writing. In a period when LGBTQ studies and queer theory were coalescing but not yet established, *OUT/LOOK* built a bridge between academic inquiry and broader community.

The Q+ Public book series was initially conceived by E. G. Crichton and Jeffrey Escoffier, two of the six founders of *OUT/LOOK*. They brought together a diverse and highly qualified editorial collective. The plan is to issue several books a year in which engaged research, art, and critical reflection address difficult and challenging topics.

The idea of a complicated and radical queer public has long been part of the vision and writing of Jeffrey Escoffier. Sadly, Jeffrey died unexpectedly in May 2022 at age seventy-nine, leaving behind Q+ Public, as well as several other publishing projects. Prolific, full of ideas and vision to the end, he is widely missed. The Q+ Public collective continues this work in his honor.

Each book in the Q+ Public series finds a way to dive into the deep nuances and discomforts of a topic. Each book features multiple points of view, strong art, and a strong editorial concept.

Criminalized Lives: HIV and Legal Violence uses fieldwork, interviews, and drawing to explore the daily lives of HIV-positive individuals who are entangled in the Canadian criminal justice system. Stigmatized by the disease and often registered as sex offenders, these are people for whom the crime of allegedly not telling sexual partners their HIV status has most often been represented by official channels: the police, media, courts, universities, and community-based HIV organizations. In contrast, this book highlights the voices and real-life stories told by the individuals themselves. What emerges is the missing picture of how the criminalization of HIV status follows longstanding racist, classist, homophobic, and colonial patterns in which people already marginalized bear the brunt of law and its enforcement. This is a story about violence rendered natural and normal because it is perpetrated from within the legal system. This book offers an intervention by presenting points of view of the victims themselves.

E. G. Crichton

Foreword

HIV criminalization is the discriminatory prosecution and imprisonment of people living with HIV for acts that would otherwise be legal or considered only minor crimes for people who have not tested HIV positive—for example, consensual sex or spitting at someone. Dozens of states and U.S. territories have HIV-specific criminal laws, including sentence enhancements for sex workers who test positive for HIV. Two types of behavior are primarily targeted: first, sexual contact without prior disclosure of HIV-positive status (may include vaginal, anal, or oral sex but is often defined to include activities posing no or low risk of HIV transmission) and, second, spitting, biting, or other modes of exposure to bodily fluids (often specific to law enforcement or correction officers). People living with HIV are also prosecuted under general criminal laws, like in Canada, for example, for aggravated sexual assault or attempted homicide.[1]

In most cases, states classify HIV laws as felony punishment, which may lead to hefty fines and other criminal penalties such as severe sentences. At least six states—Arkansas, Louisiana, Ohio, South Dakota, Tennessee, and Washington—may require years or lifetime registration on the sex offense registry.[2] For example, more than 150 people are on the Tennessee sex offense registry for HIV convictions.

Additionally, all prosecutions of U.S. military service members for HIV-related offenses fall under federal law, such as the Uniform Code of Military Justice, which does not include any provision explicitly addressing HIV transmission or exposure. Instead, military service members living with HIV face prosecution under general criminal assault provisions, similar to the criminal assault prosecution of civilians with HIV under state law, or the situation in Canada.[3]

I am a twenty-year long-term survivor who, in 2003, was diagnosed HIV positive while attempting to enlist in the U.S. military. I wasn't allowed to serve because of my HIV-positive status. My journey to liberation and activism in the domestic HIV movement began after my life was interrupted again, but this time by a grossly unjust HIV prosecution in 2009. A former partner, with whom I had a contentious relationship, and I stopped seeing each other. The partner, who had previously threatened to file charges against me for alleged failure to share my status, then went to the police and did so. At the age of thirty, I was convicted under Louisiana's so-called Intentional Exposure to AIDS Virus felony statute. I opted to take a plea rather than risk a ten-year sentence at trial. I served six months of hard labor in a South Louisiana prison and was subjected to the Sex Offense Registry for fifteen years. It was a consensual sexual relationship, and it was never determined that I transmitted HIV to anyone.

My situation is not rare. Hundreds of prosecutions throughout the southern states and all over the United States disproportionately impact socially and politically vulnerable communities already at a heightened risk of incarceration and most affected by HIV—Black, Indigenous, people of color, gay and bisexual men, women, sex workers, people who use drugs, transgender women and men, immigrants, migrants, and youth. A prosecution or an investigation related to HIV status and sensationalized media attention may lead to violations of confidentiality, privacy, job loss, housing insecurity, difficult family relationships, and custody arrangements, inflicting long-lasting individual and group harm.

Furthermore, more harm than good is done regarding the well-being, health, and safety of our communities. Criminalization laws work against responses to HIV. It punishes people living with HIV for knowing their HIV status. Criminalization creates mistrust of health professionals to protect the confidentiality of their patients. The context created by criminalization undercuts the most basic message about sexual health: ultimately, we must be collectively responsible for our actions and behaviors. However, criminalization of HIV ends up giving HIV-negative people a false sense of security, putting the onus of responsibility solely on those living with HIV.

Not only that, but HIV criminalization also works against ending the epidemic. Despite progress over the past forty years of the HIV and AIDS epidemic, with all the scientific breakthroughs, the criminal status of HIV in the United States continues to exist. The Centers for Disease and Control and Prevention, the national public health agency of the United States, asserts that "although HIV remains a threat in every part of the U.S., certain populations—and parts of the country—bear the most of the burden, signaling where high-impact HIV prevention efforts must be focused."[4] Yet the National HIV Strategic Plan for 2021–2025 (HIV Plan) and Ending the HIV Epidemic Plan (EHE) advises state governments to reform or repeal HIV criminalization laws and practices but do not provide resources or requirements in their respective plans. Also, the EHE does not require its priority jurisdictions to address HIV criminalization in their plans, leaving it up to each jurisdiction to decide for themselves whether to address their HIV criminalization laws.[5]

Communities of people living with HIV demand better laws and policies to reflect public health practices that promote health and well-being of people living with HIV and that do not contribute to discrimination and stigmatization of people living with HIV. If we want people living with HIV to share their status, we must make it legally safe to do so. Today, it is not safe to do so. Now, the risk of a misunderstanding leaves every person living with HIV just one disgruntled partner away from finding themselves in a courtroom. No criminal intent or transmission is required. In most states, there are incredibly high conviction rates in HIV criminalization cases. For example, in Louisiana, Black men account for 91 percent of HIV-related arrests.[6] Many defendants may not get a fair hearing or can afford adequate legal representation. The only legal defense is if you do not know your HIV status.

With this in mind, my greatest advocacy achievement is how gratifying the collective action for HIV decriminalization continues to increase in visibility, a trend seen every year since 2012, when I began my advocacy journey. Today, I work as a consultant and thought leader in the global HIV Justice community with over a decade of expertise in decriminalization, human rights, and the intersection between equity and social justice. I have served in leadership positions with many recognized organizations—including the Elizabeth Taylor AIDS Foundation, U.S. People Living with HIV Caucus, Health Not Prisons Collective, HIV Justice Network, and co-founder of the Sero Project. I am grateful for the opportunity to lend my voice to this project, which addresses the violence of HIV criminalization and the power of collective action to effect change. To me, what makes this book important and relevant is because readers get to learn about our journey, the movement, and issues through our common lived experiences.

Globally, the main gaps and challenges remaining in the HIV response are, however, mainly due to a continued failure to uphold human rights, especially the rights of people living with HIV, including women and girls and other groups living in situations of vulnerability, and to fund and implement required interventions at scale, such as human rights literacy, training, and support; gender equality and prevention of violence; community-based human rights empowerment and monitoring; law and policy reform; and redress for harm.[7]

Therefore, we must proactively commit to creating an affirming human rights environment for people living with HIV by eliminating HIV criminalization. Moreover, the intersection of public health and the criminal legal system in the United States involves reducing negative (human) outcomes, disease, and crime, respectively.[8] But at what cost? If living with HIV is not a crime, why are so many U.S. states treating it like it is?

At the same time, the United States remains the world's leader in mass incarceration, with two million people currently in the nation's jails and prisons—a 500 percent increase over the past forty years.[9] To me, HIV criminalization is just another way to criminalize our bodies. It comes as no surprise that the state and federal response to the domestic HIV epidemic is situated within a larger context of politics and culture, including sex negativity, HIV-related stigma, racism, homophobia, transphobia, sexism, classism, and the criminalization of poverty.[10]

For this reason, it is my assertion that any response to the impact of HIV must be rooted in racial justice.[11] Racial disparities exist in both health care and the criminal legal system. The work of racial justice in the domestic HIV movement or HIV criminal law reform is not new. We must center those communities most impacted by the epidemic in leadership and decision-making and root our efforts in accountability to the communities we lead.[12] As for the use of "Treatment as Prevention" (TASP) or "Undetectable = Untransmittable" (U = U) in the criminal law context, I support the consensus that reliance on viral load or compliance with medical treatment as a basis to reform HIV criminal laws poses dangerous consequences for those who lack access to care. It also contradicts everyone's basic right to make health care decisions, including whether and when to get treatment, without running afoul of the criminal law.[13]

We can't give up on progress. The work of activist communities who are responding and resisting criminalization remains steadfast. The Health Not Prisons Collective, an intersectional national initiative launched in 2020 by the Counter Narrative Project (CNP), Positive Women's Network—USA (PWN), Sero Project, Transgender Law Center (TLC), and the U.S. Caucus of People Living with HIV (the HIV Caucus)—longtime collaborators led by, and accountable to, communities most affected by HIV criminalization in the United States. Equally important, the Black United Leadership Initiative (BULI), a Black-centered movement born out of the 2018 HIV is Not a Crime Training Academy institutes, addresses the critical need to have a Black-only space to discuss the ways different forms of oppression play out in our communities (racism, colorism, sexism, homophobia, ableism, ageism). With the realization that the majority of people today who are newly diagnosed are Black, BULI provides an opportunity to start shaping a national landscape for Black leadership in the HIV decriminalization movement by sharing the analysis on the disproportionate impact of criminalization on Black folks and preparing to link to larger movements—while building confidence as advocates.

HIV, a chronic, manageable disease, might no longer be a death sentence, but today it is still a prison sentence. Remember that stigma pushes people out of testing, prevention, and treatment and that HIV criminalization is more stigmatizing than language; it puts a target on the backs of people living with HIV.

Robert Suttle

Preface

This book emerges in context of a changing legal landscape of HIV-related criminalization in Canada. After years of dedicated activism and advocacy, led by people living with HIV and human rights campaigners, there have been new limits on prosecutions and calls for the way the Canadian Criminal Code applies to cases of HIV nondisclosure to change. Since 1989, criminal laws have been applied to the act of an HIV-positive person not telling another person their HIV-positive status, where there was a potential for transmission (namely, in the context of sex)—otherwise termed HIV nondisclosure. This approach has made Canada a global hot spot for HIV-related criminalization. In cases of HIV nondisclosure, HIV does not need to be transmitted. Rather, it is the act of not telling the other person one's HIV-positive status that is criminalized. Under Canadian criminal law, in a precedent we inherited as a settler state of the British empire, when someone garners sex via a fraud, the other person's consent to sex is vitiated, or cancelled. Here, the act of not telling someone else one's HIV-positive status is considered fraud. The law understands such sex in such a context as a violation, meaning laws of sexual assault could be applied, with HIV being understood as the aggravating factor. Over time, Crown prosecutors in Canada were successful at getting this precedent to relate to instances of HIV nondisclosure, and the Supreme Court agreed. This use of the law often resulted in those prosecuted being registered as sex offenders. This book is a record of the many harms that resulted from this legal trajectory, and indeed, my research was developed to help highlight the injustice done to people living with HIV under this form of criminalization.

There is a growing consensus to no longer use the laws of sexual assault to certain instances of HIV nondisclosure. In 2019, the House of Commons Standing Committee on Justice and Human Rights, a federal body governing changes to Canadian criminal laws, recommended to immediately end the use of sexual assault laws in cases of HIV nondisclosure. The minister of justice heeded these calls and mobilized, however slowly, to introduce Criminal Code reform to remedy some of the harms of what they call the "overcriminalization" of HIV nondisclosure. With the laws in flux, there may well soon be some minimal changes, which limit the scope of harms resulting from criminalization. But what history tells us is that whatever changes are made will not be good enough in a society that relies on the horrors of legal violence to manage complexity and difference. Until the foundations of the system itself are undone, forms of legal violence will continue to manifest, justifying myriad forms of other violence.

With the laws of sexual assault potentially no longer in play, HIV nondisclosure will be criminalized using some sort of less severe charge, but a charge nonetheless. Limiting the violence of a prosecution of aggravated sexual assault, the sex offender registry, and deportations for noncitizens will be a major success. But with a minimalist approach to limit the scope of harms of criminalization, the slogan mobilized by activists around the world—*HIV Is Not a Crime*—will continue to be untrue in Canada.

As with any process of reforms, as concessions are made, or demands come to be watered down, concerns are emerging that things might backfire or that, with a turn away from forms of punishment, this could widen the scope of surveillance and control from public health authorities. In 2018, the federal minister of justice, implementing a directive to limit charges related to HIV nondisclosure under federal jurisdiction (primarily only over a limited area in the Canadian north), stated that prosecutors should "consider whether public health authorities have provided services to a person living with HIV who has not disclosed their HIV status prior to sexual activity when determining whether it is in the public interest to pursue a prosecution."[1] Less of a reliance on criminal laws could mean a greater reliance on coercive public health approaches, including issuing legal orders that mandate medical monitoring, and forms of public health policy and practice where public health officials and police act in concert to govern HIV prevention.

However, as this book illustrates, and as antipoverty and AIDS activist Gary Kinsman has stated, people living with HIV are not the public in public health.[2] In a context where the public health system was established as part of the ongoing project of settler colonization, many people living with HIV across Canada—particularly those who are marginalized due to racism, Indigeneity, migration status, sexuality, gender identity, use of drugs deemed illegal, and past or current engagement in sex work and/or the criminal legal system—live in a context of fear and uncertainty when it comes to engaging with health care and public health authorities.

So, while HIV-related criminalization may be somewhat limited in scope, minimizing some harms, Canadian settler-colonial law and the ongoing patterns of social inequality that result remain intact. This book presents a record of the past and ongoing harms of criminalization and lessons from advocacy calling for reform and transformation. My intention is to put into question the ways in which the criminal legal system and public health institutions work (or, rather, do not work) for people. Despite a focus solely on HIV criminalization, my hope is that these histories and experiences will underscore the problems of all forms of criminalization, be them related to sex and sexuality, drugs, poverty, citizenship status, or otherwise. In a context of increasing inequality, a turning tide toward populist tough-on-crime agendas, and rising hate crimes, the concerns raised in this book are more relevant than ever.

In developing this book, I have several people to thank who made this work possible. Specifically, I would like to thank all the people who trusted me with their stories. Thank you for sharing your experiences and allowing me into your lives to bear witness. This project is dedicated to all of you in your ongoing efforts to seek peace and justice.

I want to thank Eric Koustik Williams for his illustrations to help bring humanity to this topic. I want to thank Robert Suttle for helping elaborate the U.S. context of HIV criminalization in the foreword. Thank you to Q+ Public, especially Andy Spieldenner, E. G. Crichton, and the late Jeffery Escoffier, for taking a chance on this book. I would like to thank Sarah Flicker for encouraging me to engage in academic research and to Viviane Namaste for thoughtfully mentoring me to become an academic researcher. Much gratitude for your guidance along the way to Martin French, Chris Bruckert, and Michael Orsini. I owe deep thanks to Nick Boyce, Zoë Dodd, Mikiki, Jordan Arseneault, and Jessica Whitbread for supporting me through developing this work. Thank you to those I have learned so much from in helping me conceive of the ideas in this book, including, Chad Clarke, Michelle Whonnock, Eric Mykhalovskiy, Stephen Molldrem, Sarah Schulman, Richard Elliot, Ryan Peck, Maureen Owino, Trevor Hoppe, Colin Hastings, Joshua Pavan, Eli Manning, Sean Strub, Steven Trasher, and Theodore Kerr. Thanks to Madi Haslam for support in reviewing and thank you Avital Cherniawsky for your work on the index. I would also like to thank community and advocacy organizations who helped make my research possible, including Prisoners AIDS Support Action Network (PASAN), HIV and AIDS Legal Clinic of Ontario (HALCO), *Sisters* of *Fire* at Ka Ni Kanichihk, the HIV Legal Network, the SERO Project, the HIV Justice Network, and the Canadian Coalition to Reform HIV Criminalization. My research was made possible through doctoral research funding from the Canadian Institutes of Health Research (CIHR), and this book was made possible with funding from Carleton University, Faculty of Public Affairs.

Acronyms

AIDS	acquired immunodeficiency syndrome
DNA	deoxyribonucleic acid
HAART	highly active antiretroviral therapy
HIV	human immunodeficiency virus
PTSD	posttraumatic stress disorder
RCMP	Royal Canadian Mounted Police
SOR	sex offender registry
STBBI	sexually transmitted blood-borne infection

Criminalized Lives

FIG. 1.1. Title illustration

~ 1 ~

Bearing Witness to Violence

This is a book about violence. Violence that is rendered natural and normal because it is the product of a legal outcome. Violence that reduces living subjects with autonomy and dignity to objects of persecution, punishment, and condemnation. Violence that is enacted out of morality, ignorance, hatred, and misunderstanding. Violence that is deeply rooted in the racist legacy of settler-colonial state institutions. Specifically, this book is about the violence that results from criminalizing the human immunodeficiency virus (HIV). HIV is a common human experience. Over 30 million people around the world live with HIV. In many places, due to access to antiretroviral medications, HIV has been rendered a chronic and long-term condition where people can live out the full course of natural lives. In this context of criminalization and medical advances, the only harm that will come to some people living with HIV today is not from the virus itself but rather from social institutions like police, criminal courts, and prisons.

For years, I have been a witness to the harms of criminalizing HIV, as an activist and a researcher. I have had HIV my entire adult life. I tested HIV positive in 1997, at nineteen years old, a year after the breakthrough introduction of life-saving highly active antiretroviral therapies (HARRTs), which dramatically transformed the ongoing crisis for some. This was the era, which Alexandra Juhasz and Ted Kerr call the "second silence,"[1] where from 1996 to 2008, while an ongoing crisis, HIV began to take up less space in the public sphere and became less visible in dominant frames of knowing and understanding the world. While HARRT began to curb the massive death rate in North America, my doctor told me I would not live past thirty years old, and a public health nurse told me to refrain from sex altogether. While I have known my whole adult life with HIV, I also have never known a sex life outside of fears of surveillance, policing, and criminalization. The summer I tested HIV positive, the national news had a story about a man being criminally charged for not telling a sex partner that he was HIV positive. The following year, I started working at a peer support program for other young people living with HIV. I became a peer support worker, running education programs on healthy sexuality and living with HIV for other urban young people with the virus.

A few years into my time at the organization, one of the peers who came to the program, and whom I considered a friend, had been arrested. He was facing charges of aggravated sexual assault for having consensual sex. HIV was not transmitted, yet his partner's fears of HIV drove him to call the police. I was called by his lawyer and was asked to testify if it went to court. The young man who had been arrested had only recently learned he had HIV and had come to the safer sex and living with HIV workshops I put on. His lawyer thought I could support his case. This case sent a shockwave of fear through our small community. We were trying to cope with life with the virus, to take care of each other and our sex partners. Yet, the police, media and court's story of what happened dominated. Our friend was labeled a perpetrator of harm and charged with aggravated sexual assault, his name blasted across newspapers and online. He was banished from social media and public life in his community. The mark of accusation, in a context of silence, fear, and stigma, quickly undid any sense of support we had been working to build. Our friend was put under house arrest. His account and understanding of what happened to him erased and denied.

The case of my friend was unfortunately not unique. When someone is criminalized with a morally signified crime, such as those related to HIV, they can quickly lose the right to share their own account of what happened. Their story is sensationalized and told for them by police, courts, and media. The accused is denied access to autonomy and privacy and is often framed as a violent perpetrator who has intentionally aimed to "spread" HIV to others and thus needs intervention and incapacitation via forms of state-sanctioned violence. Through the dichotomous victim versus perpetrator logic of the criminal legal system, the process of criminalization transforms people into objects of risk and threat. The blunt violence of the criminal law flattens complexity and nuance, which limits our collective understanding of how these cases came about in the first place.

Despite the realities of living with the virus today, a legacy of moral signification means that HIV is still a highly stigmatized disease that is heavily regulated by the criminal legal system. According to the global advocacy group, the HIV Justice Network, both Canada and the United States have long been known as global "hot spots" for criminalizing HIV, where, depending on the jurisdiction, exposure to the virus, or the act of not disclosing one's HIV-positive status to sexual partners, can be a serious criminal offence.[2] Such offences can lead to long periods of incarceration, sensationalistic media coverage, registration as a sex offender, and daily forms of stigma, discrimination, and violence. In addition to criminal laws, public health laws can also be mobilized to increase surveillance, regulation, and enforcement of people's sex lives and treatment adherence. Research and experience underline that the criminalization of HIV follows longstanding racist, classist, homophobic, and colonial patterns, where people already made marginalized and oppressed bear the brunt of laws and their enforcement.

When starting this project, I asked myself the question: how do we know what we know about the criminalization of HIV? When answering this question, it became clear that most often what counted as knowledge on this issue came from institutional, expert, and official ways of knowing. Ways of knowing from the police, media, courts, universities, and community-based HIV organizations. Much focus in literature has been on the specifics of legal interpretation,[3] on the negative impact of criminalization on public health[4,5] and HIV responses,[6] or on the cultural impact of HIV criminalization.[7] Less attention has been paid on the backend of the criminal legal system and what results from legal doctrine in the daily lives of people or on the impact of movements calling for change.

As feminist scholar Viviane Namaste points out, with the recent prominence of AIDS history and cultural revisitation circulating in the public sphere, a dominant focus has been on telling the past of gay white male communities.[8] In examining the often-ignored historical impact of HIV on Haitian communities in Montreal, Canada, Namaste aims to counter the rise of dominant narratives and calls for the epistemological intervention of studying knowledge "otherwise" about the history of AIDS. Knowledge otherwise being that which is unexplored, erased, or ignored. There is increasing proliferation of knowledge development into the histories of HIV and AIDS otherwise. For example, Alexandra Juhasz and Theodore Kerr have been exploring why AIDS is remembered and known through American cultural production,[9] and Marika Cifor has been examining AIDS nostalgia, the archive, and memory of AIDS and its documentation by activist communities.[10] Now, in accounts of the past of HIV and AIDS community mobilization, greater nuance and understanding are coming to light, of which Sarah Schulman's nuanced account of the complex and diverse histories of women and people of color involved in ACT UP New York is a prime example.[11] As is the recent edited collection *AIDS and the Distribution of Crises*, from editors Jih-Fei Cheng, Alexandra Juhasz, and Nishant Shahani, which aims to displace dominant ways of knowing the AIDS crisis as being situated in one community and at a historical time in the past.[12] My work here follows the call from Namaste to account for the histories and present of AIDS *otherwise*.

My research began with another question: What are the daily experiences of HIV-positive people who have been engaged in the criminal legal system because they allegedly did not tell their sexual partner(s) that they are HIV positive? To answer this question, I spent two years undertaking fieldwork with people who are at the center of HIV criminalization cases across Canada. With a focus on the daily lives of HIV-positive people in Canada who have been charged, prosecuted, and incarcerated—many of whom are now registered sex offenders—for allegedly not telling sexual partners that they have the virus. Findings from my research disarticulate criminalized people from dominant narratives of guilt, innocence, and redemption, which are commonly put forth as justifications for violence. Instead, what I found calls attention toward forms of suffering that criminalized people faced within and outside of the criminal legal and public health systems.

In speaking directly with people who have been criminally charged, we can put into question the dominant understanding held by police, courts, public health authorities, and the media that people living with HIV are violent perpetrators who are actively trying to transmit the virus to others. Rather, what comes to be institutionally understood as wrongdoing is much less obviously so. The criminal legal system forces complex and nuanced situations—including the realities of people's silence, fear, actual disclosure, or, in some cases, their inability to address their own HIV status—into the dichotomous narrative of victim/perpetrator.

My research is a gesture of undoing and resistance, aiming to intervene in mainstream ways of knowing people living with HIV as vectors of disease and perpetrators of harm. In doing so, I ask ongoing questions: Why, in Canada, is HIV regulated so harshly? What if the people who are targets of HIV criminalization are not the public safety risk they are perceived to be? What if they themselves were survivors of violence? What if the victim/perpetrator logic is too reductive to understand the complexity of communicable disease transmission and human social and sexual relationships? And how do we contend with the

FIG. 1.2. Field research and illustration process

deeply embedded racism, homophobia, and misogyny that drives criminalization?

Illustrations

Throughout this book, I present a series of real-life stories collected from my research, linking the stories to archival findings and presenting them alongside comic illustrations of queer comic artist Eric Kostiuk Williams. The characters in this book were developed out of composite experiences of the twenty-seven in-depth qualitative interviews I conducted with sixteen people (four cis women, one trans woman, and eleven cis men) across five provinces in Canada. These people are from diverse backgrounds who comprise a wide range of experiences across the spectrum of who has faced criminal charges and public health orders in relation to HIV nondisclosure, including those who are socially marginalized, Black and Indigenous people, gay men, women with histories of street-based sex work, and people who live poverty. The stories people shared with me are focused on the complex and violent experience of being criminalized.

None of the illustrations are intended to look like the actual people I interviewed, and we used the approach as a form of visual pseudonym. The main characters in this book are representative of the range of experiences I collected. To protect the confidentiality of the people I interviewed, names and places have been changed, but the experiences and quotes are directly from people I interviewed. To further protect confidentiality, in some instances, stories from more than one person have been brought together into one character in this book. However, no details on demographics were changed, except for in some instances age and location. To protect the dignity and integrity of the people,

FIG. 1.3. Shaun portrait

I did not change someone's self-identified race, gender, or sexuality.

The aim of this research, and linking the stories and illustrations, is to bring understanding, dignity, humanity, and a sense of justice to situations where no justice was done. And while this book is about violence, it is also about resistance to violence and movements calling for change. To counter the way criminalized people are popularly understood through dominant narratives, Eric worked to bring joy, nuance, complexity, and a sense of realness to their portraits.

SHAUN

Shaun is in his late twenties. He is from the island of St. Vincent and the Grenadines in the Caribbean. He moved to Canada to go to college and lives in the suburbs with his dog. He has been living with HIV for three years.

CYNTHIA

Cynthia is in her forties. She lives downtown. She moved undocumented to Canada from Mexico to live her life as a woman. She enjoys her work as a sex worker. She has lived with HIV for one year.

FIG. 1.4. Cynthia portrait

FIG. 1.5. Lenore portrait

LENORE

Lenore is in her early thirties. She lives in the Canadian prairies with her boyfriend. She wants to be a hairdresser. She found out she is HIV positive four years ago.

MATTEO

Matteo is in his early twenties. He loves the gay village and enjoys going out to bars with his friends. He is a student. He found out he is HIV positive three years ago.

FIG. 1.6. Matteo portrait

Criminalization as Violence

Before moving forward, two central phenomena need to be defined—violence and criminalization. I discuss both in the following section.

VIOLENCE

Violence is not a mere concept or theory, but a material reality faced by people. Enactments of violence can be systematized and highly organized, or random and arbitrary. In examining the complexities and nuances in enactments of violence, scholars, such as political philosopher Hannah Arendt, have sought to explicate violence more broadly than simply a single blow from one individual person to another. Instead, Arendt explored how violence is used as an instrument of nation-states serving to maintain forms of power and authority. Arendt, who was concerned about fascism and totalitarianism, notes that when violence appears, it is because a hold on power is in jeopardy.[13] Anticolonial philosopher Frantz Fanon examined the role of violence in the context of imperialism and colonization, whereby violence is mobilized to construct a dichotomy between the colonizer/colonized, the civilized/barbarian, the respectable/degenerate, the human/subhuman, and to humanize/racialize.[14] Philosopher Walter Benjamin helped conceptualize the notion of legal violence, or violence that is legitimized by nation-states. Benjamin sought to understand how certain forms of violence are deemed legitimate, while others are deemed illegitimate, as well as how lines are drawn between the two. By legal violence, Benjamin meant sanctioned violence, and when talking about law, he was referring to European legal frameworks and tools. Benjamin elaborated that legal violence served two functions: lawmaking and law-preserving. Lawmaking violence represents the means resulting in new laws or a new legal system being put into place, whereas law-preserving violence is that harnessed to preserve the existence of the current legal system. In Benjamin's analysis, the nation-state is the only official bearer of legitimate violence and the arbiter of forms of violence deemed legitimate and illegitimate.[15]

Legal violence is rationalized, wielded solely by the nation-state as a form of punishment, risk management, and an act of retribution, enacted on people because they have been convicted of breaking state laws. Legal violence, then, is understood as a rational and measured outcome to lawbreaking and is regularly conflated with the notion of justice. In some cases, the acceptability of legal violence remains contested, such as with solitary confinement, which has been deemed to be torture by many experts, yet in some countries can still be rendered legal under certain conditions.

Removing someone's autonomy, limiting their right to liberty, and marking them as a risk to the safety of others, to be under heightened surveillance, are forms of violence that comprise the unmaking of a person through law. These forms of legal violence come to organize the lives of people who are criminalized in relation to HIV. This makes possible a whole array of other forms of violence, or forms of extralegal violence, which extend beyond formal institutional punishments into a broad range of populist forms of violent retribution, social marginalization, and discrimination.

Sociologist and mathematician Johan Galtung, instrumental in establishing the field of peace and conflict studies, conceived of the notion of structural violence.[16] Galtung defines peace as the absence of violence. But his definition of violence is not quite so simple. Violence for Galtung exists "when human beings are being influenced so that their actual somatic and mental realizations are below their potential realization." Therefore, violence is here defined as "the cause of the difference between the potential and the actual."[17] In other words, if someone's potential to flourish is limited due to an avoidable action or circumstance, that could be defined as violence. Galtung uses the example of life expectancy, noting that during the Neolithic period, a life expectancy of thirty years would not represent an expression of violence. This life expectancy contemporarily would, however, stand as an expression of violence, as protective measures to prevent death, including enabling access to medicines and healthcare were inhibited, thus signaling inequality and social disparities. But, when an outcome is unavoidable, violence, according to Galtung, is not present. If the actual is avoidable, then violence is present.

Criminologist Carmella Murdocca names that manifestations of structural violence are "squarely in the material" and notes that in Canada, a country founded on settler-colonial values of racial purity and morality, structural violence is always constituted by racism and linked to forms of nationalism.[18] In Canada, the normative order of society is maintained through colonial laws, customs, and ways of being, which is maintained through the enactment of legal violence. Legal violence as a form of structural violence maintains the status quo to uphold colonial ways of being and knowing.

This structural understanding of violence has enabled threads of analysis from criminology to queer theory. For example, queer theorist and prison abolitionist Eric Stanley, who, in examining the social marginalization of racialized queer and trans people under regimes of criminalization and social exclusion, notes that "thinking of violence as individual acts versus epistemic force works to support a normative and normalizing structuring of pain." [19] But through social systems, bureaucracies, and institutions, violence can be obscured, a process Stanley notes as the "privatization of violence," where violence against racialized queer and trans people is obfuscated from public view, lacking accountability, oversight, or public understanding.

Indeed, contemporary forms of incarceration are an act of privatizing violence, where all incarcerated people experience the legal violence of punishment hidden from public view. Criminologist David Garland has argued that the disappearing body is one way that contemporary state punishment, both carceral and capital, can maintain its legitimacy and control. Garland has sought to address the range of bodily "pains of imprisonment."[20] In his work, Garland studied double bunking and the *Brown v. Plata* case, upheld by the Supreme Court of the United States, resulting in California having to reduce the number of incarcerated individuals. Photographic evidence presented showed fifty prisoners were held in a 12-by-20–foot cage awaiting medical treatment, and prisoners have been held in telephone booth–sized cages for long periods of time without access to toilets. Garland also examined the practice of lethal injection and the use of the drug pancuronium bromide, which had no therapeutic purpose and only suppressed bodily movements at the time of death to avoid discomfort for the audience. In examining these forms of hidden violence and to counter the privatization of violence, Garland hoped to make the body visible, and the legal violence enacted against the body as undeniably present and something with which society must contend.

Following these threads of analysis and conceptions of violence, and by sharing the stories of criminalized people, I will examine legal and extralegal types of violence in the context of HIV criminalization to begin the work of denaturalizing the violence of criminalization. The aim of denaturalizing violence is to understand people's suffering as not merely an inevitable matter of fate but as the result of social and structural processes. The notion of "denaturalization" in relation to violence comes from the work of critical social science scholar and critical realist Andrew Sayer.[21] Denaturalization is not about revealing some formerly hidden or deliberately concealed truth. Rather, the aim is to present a critique against forms of oppressive social organization that result in people's suffering. Specifically, Sayer focuses on forms of avoidable suffering that occur because of social systems. This approach moves the scope of social research away from solely contending with theoretical ideas. This approach avoids conceptual debates about what constitutes truth and instead the focus is attuned to the material and forms of avoidable suffering and injustice in the actual world. Here, attention is placed on understanding how social phenomena do not need to remain the same and are constantly open to and subject to change, with an ethical view that another world is possible. Examining the ways in which the violence of criminalization operates is not done solely for the sake of documenting. Rather, this understanding seeks to contribute to critiques challenging the administration of punishment in society, to bear witness, and to call for action. Perhaps most of all, this approach aims to serve to form the political basis of a life worth living—one of flourishing—for people who have been subject to all forms of criminalization, including those related to HIV.

CRIMINALIZATION

No group of people is inherently criminal. Rather, criminalization is a shifting process that targets certain people at certain times for certain purposes. The shifting nature of the criminalization of HIV aligns with a constructivist understanding of "the law," as elaborated by scholars Nikolas Rose and Mariana Valverde. They argue the law is not a "unified phenomenon governed by certain principles" but rather a social, political, economic construction that can be applied to regulate aspects of society at specific moments in time.[22] Viewed through this lens, the criminalization of HIV has been actively negotiated and put in place historically by a wide range of actors and institutions.

Criminalization is deeply intertwined and co-constituted with conceptions of race and colonization. Anthropologist Sally Engle Merry notes that criminalization is "the reinterpretation of everyday behaviour as an offence against the state."[23] This understanding of criminalization is of vital importance in the context of settler colonization, where criminalization of everyday life was imagined and implemented by those in power to promote certain ways of being and doing—those that promoted settler purity and order. In Canada, very plainly this meant to advance the project of colonization, Indigenous ways of life—speaking language, practicing culture, custom, and tradition—were actively criminalized. Abolitionist scholar Robin Maynard, has examined Canada's history of colonization and slavery, and the historic establishment and deployment of policing forces which were intended to enforce white settler order.[24] This history feeds directly into present-day realities of racial injustice and the disproportionate forms of criminalization.

When a form of criminalization targets a specific population of people, members of that group must live their lives in the shadow of the law and can be subject to legal violence. Punishment—the most common form of legal violence—in Canada, as in most places with a common law tradition, acts to deconstitute the personhood of people labeled criminal. Many groups of people are rendered as those who must *live in a negative relation to the law*: people living with feared diseases; those without legal status; Black and Indigenous and other racialized people; people who live in poverty; people with differing abilities; those who are neurodivergent; those who sell or buy drugs, or sell or buy sex; people who are sexual minorities; those who are trans; and those who live in neighborhoods under increased police surveillance—the list goes on.

As legal philosopher Colin Dayan notes, living in a negative relation to the law means one's legally granted rights to personhood can be easily deconstituted.[25] Dayan explored a genealogy of what she calls negative forms of personhood, such as criminals, slaves, detainees, and animals. Negative forms of personhood are historically constituted through an array of legal processes. Legal protections, such as rights to autonomy, freedom of movement, economic security, civic engagement, and privacy, which are granted to those living in a positive relation to the law, are stripped away from those in a negative relation through forms of state-sanctioned violence, surveillance, and incapacitation. Looking back to ancient common law, Dayan noted that there were three principal outcomes of criminality via treason or felony: (1) the forfeiture of property to the sovereign; (2) the corruption of blood, which blocked the descent of property, cutting off inheritance and blood ties; and (3) the extinction of civil rights, resulting in the incapacity to perform any legal function. Blood and property were regarded as metaphors constituting persons in civil society, and thus the corruption of blood and forfeiture of property came to be "operative components of divestment" in personhood. A lack of legal protections that enable personhood can mean a person is reduced solely to the biology of the human body, resembling the subhuman, what philosopher Giorgio Agamben calls "homo sacer," or bare life.[26]

But what exactly constitutes personhood? For philosophers, this question is not one of biology. Being alive in a biological sense does not alone constitute personhood. Rather, a person is composed of a series of attributes, for example, freedom of will and desire to act in certain ways—to be different, to work, to be an individual who makes choices, to make moral judgments, to speak for oneself.

In nation-states founded on liberal ideals, such as Canada and the United States, some of these attributes are enabled through legal frameworks, such as a national constitution that guarantees freedom of expression, speech, and mobility to its citizens. In this sense, the person represents a liberal invention, and legal frameworks help enable access to the mechanisms that facilitate and protect civil life for persons.

In the legal context, claims for personhood are often framed as claims for civilly enabled human rights. Thus, the language of human rights can be understood as the language of personhood. This language comprises a wide array of social processes, systems, ideas, and tools, including the law and legal frameworks. Many of these things that enable personhood are invisible, such as the legal frameworks guaranteeing the right to live a life free from harm. They operate on an invisible theoretical plane around the natural biological attributes of the body.

The production of personhood also produces the possibility of its negative: the nonperson or animal. By defining positive personhood, legal processes also define its opposite, negative personhood. In defining the human rights of certain subjects, the language of rights continually negatively constitutes nonrights. As philosopher Roberto Esposito notes, "The person not only includes its own proper negative within it, but constantly reproduces the negative."[27] Inherent to the notion of a person, Esposito argues, is the nonperson—a subject denied access to self-determination and autonomy. Forms of liberal politics that emerge from this process include the safeguarding of rights of certain persons predicated on the suspension of the rights of others. A concern here is that a reliance on rights-based politics results in both the deserving of rights and the undeserving of rights. In positive rights, negative rights are co-constituted. In examining the experience of social death of undocumented people, scholar Lisa Marie Cacho argues that conceptions of personhood in America are founded on the disposition and exploitation of criminalized people of color.[28]

Under regimes of criminalization, certain groups can come to be easily stripped of legal personhood and placed under heightened forms of surveillance and regulation simply because of who they are and how they live their lives. The criminalized population is marked as "other" and loses the ability to participate in aspects of society granted to citizens.

In the context of sexuality and criminalization, feminist sexualities scholar Gayle Rubin has famously noted in 1984 that "sex is presumed guilty until proven innocent," underlining how sex and fears surrounding sex and sexuality are intensified and moralized, and how quickly someone deemed a deviant regarding sex and sexuality can be socially isolated, surveilled, and incapacitated, regardless of legal processes.[29]

In Canada and the United States, homosexual sex and ways of life have been active targets of criminalization. Joey Mogul, Andrea Ritchie, and Kay Whitlock note that fears of queers as "disease spreaders" and criminals who exist outside of heterosexual morality and norms have resulted in intensified forms of policing of queer life.[30] In Canada, in 1969, two provisions in the Criminal Code—"buggery" and "gross indecency"—were adapted to add an exception clause that allowed such acts between only two consenting adults in private. This came to be framed by some as the decriminalization of homosexuality in Canada. At the time, then Prime Minister Trudeau said publicly, "There's no place for the state in the bedrooms of the nation." However, after this change, forms of policing and criminalization targeting the queer community intensified. Queer activist sociologist Gary Kinsman and queer historian Tom Hooper have underlined that after 1969, charges for consensual queer sex increased—specifically, the criminalization of sex in queer spaces, as large mass arrests in bathhouses and public cruising spaces took place in Montreal, Toronto, Ottawa, Edmonton, Calgary, and other cities across the country.[31] Following the work of Rubin, stigma, fears, and policing responses to sex and sexuality have been dubbed the "War on Sex" by queer sexualities scholar David Halperin and sociologist Trevor Hoppe, who examine the ways forms of stigmatized sex and sexuality are regulated by law, surveillance, and social control.[32]

When fears surrounding sex, communicable disease, and criminality intersect, forms of state criminalization are amplified. The term *viral underclass* was first deployed by AIDS activist Sean Strub, who is living with HIV, to address living in a negative relation to the law as HIV-positive people under regimes of criminalization.[33] Journalist and scholar Steven Thrasher has articulated an expansive version of the concept, examining how racialization, criminalization, and ongoing crises of communicable disease intertwine and intersect to create a viral underclass, whereby entire sectors of society are left in precarity, under surveillance, policed, and excluded. Thrasher articulates criminalization as intertwined with capitalism, where poor and racialized people are left to fend for themselves in a vacuum of social supports yet are governed only via forms of coercion and incapacitation. Under a capitalist organization of society, a context of intensified dispossession, yet intensified forms of policing and surveillance, is what geographer and prison abolitionist Ruth Wilson Gilmore calls "organized abandonment."[34] This is a process of purposeful neglect, framing people as surplus to the contemporary political economic order. Organized abandonment as criminalization flourishes in times of crisis, where instead of supports, forms of incapacitation, surveillance, and social control are deployed. Scholar Karma Chavez has outlined how borders operate to exclude and criminalize in times of crisis, and how fear of AIDS and racist scapegoating of racialized migrants in the United States led to calls for quarantine, deportations, and a twenty-year immigration and travel ban for people living with HIV entering the country.[35] Chavez outlines how in 1987, after the U.S.

Congress passed legislation defining HIV as a "dangerous and contagious disease," Guantanamo Bay was used to forcibly quarantine Haitian migrants living with HIV in an open-air detention center, some for more than a year.

Criminalization pervades all aspects of the lives of those who live in a negative relation to the law, where states of exception, social inclusion, and the deconstitution of personhood become normalized in daily life for migrants, queers, people of color, and those on the margins.[36] When a person living with HIV is no longer being regarded as a person who is protected under legal regimes, they live a life in a negative relation to the law, facing criminal or public health sanctions and must live a life under constant threat. They are overpoliced, underprotected, and surveilled in their communities. Information about them is collected, exposed, dispersed, and mobilized to incapacitate their bodies and circumscribe their opportunities.

Criminalizing HIV

Both Canada and the United States have become well known for criminalizing people who have allegedly not disclosed their HIV-positive status to sexual partners or who have exposed someone to potential HIV transmission through other means. There are over 65,000 people living with HIV in Canada, of whom more than 240 have been prosecuted in relation to allegations of HIV nondisclosure.[37] Similar to the United States, Canada has concentrated HIV epidemics among subsets of the population, including gay and bisexual men, Black people, Indigenous people, and people who inject drugs.

Unlike Canada, where there is one Criminal Code and general criminal laws are used to criminalize HIV, in the

United States, each state has different criminal laws, and either general criminal laws governing crimes such as assault, attempted murder, or reckless endangerment or HIV-specific laws are applied. Over thirty states and territories specifically criminalize HIV exposure through sex, shared injection equipment, or "bodily fluids" that can include saliva (despite the scientific impossibility of HIV to be transmitted via saliva). Punishments differ across states, ranging from fines of $1,000 to incarceration of up to thirty years. In Missouri, although never applied, the HIV-specific law allows for the death penalty if transmission is proven because of HIV exposure without disclosure. States also have sentence enhancements, meaning the intensity of an existing charge and sentence can be increased if a person is known to have HIV, such as the charge of aggravated prostitution in Tennessee.

Since its first manifestations, the criminalization process in relation to HIV was, and continues to be, a highly racialized and gendered phenomenon, with a disproportionate number of Black, Indigenous, and people of color being impacted. Most recent research from the Canadian-based HIV Legal Network indicates that between 2012 and 2016, almost half of all people charged for whom race is known were Black men. Additionally, Indigenous women in Canada account for a large proportion of women charged, with at least 38 percent of women charged being Indigenous—when race or ethnicity is known.[38] Beyond the issue of racialized disproportionate representation in charges and prosecutions, sociologists Colin Hastings and Eric Mykhalovskiy have outlined how Black men bear the brunt of media reporting on HIV criminalization cases, which amplifies racist stereotypes,[39] and scholar Eli Manning is working on forthcoming research that underlines that racialized people face harsher sentences. In analyzing racism in the context of

HIV criminalization, Manning has also further outlined how Black people have been historically cast as a monstrous other in the public sphere—a logic that underwrites ongoing colonization and the white supremacy in both public health response and the criminal legal system.[40] Yet, still popular misconceptions of AIDS linger, and the idea that HIV and, as a result, its criminalization, have solely impacted gay white men is commonplace. Over the years, people have often misunderstood my research to be about white gay men, based on their own assumptions on who is impacted by this issue.

Scholars Amy Sanderson, Flo Ranville, Sherri Pooyak, Andrea Krüsi, and colleagues have outlined how, in an ongoing context of colonial violence, the legal requirements of HIV nondisclosure are unattainable for Indigenous women living with HIV, who may have less access to be able to safely disclose their HIV-positive status, negotiate condom use, and maintain a low viral load.[41] The results are ongoing social isolation and exclusion, as well as lack of access to safe health care and supports.

Racialized women who had fled their country of origin for fears of HIV stigma or access to health care have also faced deportations in relation to HIV nondisclosure cases. In one instance, a woman living with HIV had been criminally prosecuted in relation to allegations of HIV nondisclosure. She argued in court that she as unaware of her HIV status, and, if deported back to Thailand, she would only have one or two years left to live because of a lack accessible medication in the country. During her three-year sentence at the Vanier Centre for Women in Milton, Ontario, her condition had developed into an advanced stage of AIDS. Yet, she was ultimately deported to Thailand after serving her sentence in 2010 by the Canada Border Services Agency.

Over the past thirty years, approaches to criminalizing HIV have been an active and ongoing site of contestation, a terrain in-flux, negotiated, and controversial in Canada.

In 2012, two cases, one from the provinces of Alberta and one from Quebec, were appealed to the Supreme Court of Canada. This followed an earlier Supreme Court decision from 1998. In 2012, the Court responded with the landmark decision that has been acting to guide the application of charges relating to HIV nondisclosure. The decision states that people are obliged to tell a partner they have HIV before they engage in sexual acts that pose a "realistic possibility" of transmission.[42]

The outcome of precedent-setting Supreme Court decisions can be what is known as a legal test. For something to meet the threshold of the law, it should have to meet the requirements of the legal test. The legal test that emerged from the 2012 decision requires sex with a condom, and the person with HIV must have a low viral load. In the absence of *both* using a condom *and* having a low viral load, without first disclosing one's serostatus, the court has reinterpreted consensual sex as nonconsensual sex. Consent under these conditions is presumed by the Court to have been vitiated or nullified, where sex then becomes constituted as fraudulent and is equated with an assault, with HIV being the aggravating factor. The underlying assumptions are that no one would ever want to sleep with someone living with HIV and that HIV can cause bodily harm. An outcome of this decision is that now one's level of viral infectiousness has been codified and linked to notions of criminality.

Since the 2012 Supreme Court ruling, there have been several cases where people have been imprisoned under charges of aggravated sexual assault, even when they were not infectious, due to taking effective antiviral medications and when there was no transmission of HIV.[43] This is because it is the act of not telling another person about HIV that is criminalized. So, people have been criminalized regardless of HIV transmission. It is the act of not telling (commonly referred to as "nondisclosure") that comes to be understood as an aggravated sexual assault—one of the harshest charges in the country's Criminal Code, with a prison sentence of up to twenty-five years. To underline the ongoing colonial legacy woven into Canada's criminal legal system, the 2012 decision relies on several precedents related to fraud, being understood to vitiate consent from cases in the United Kingdom, including *R. v. Bennett* from 1866, which is before the confederation of Canada as a country.

A concerning flip side of the increased use of viral detectability as a measure of criminality has resulted in the intensified marginalization of those who cannot achieve viral suppression (due to access to health care, adherence and compliance to anti-HIV medications, or biological factors) and are thus understood to need increased medical and state surveillance and control. Furthermore, condom use can be out of the control of some partners, due to power differential and intimate partner violence, leaving particularly women living with HIV in a precarious position with the law.

People who are prosecuted for HIV nondisclosure with charges of aggravated sexual assault can face very long sentences, are registered as sex offenders for life, and can be held in administrative segregation when incarcerated—which means 23.5 hours per day in a cell alone under protective custody measures. The charge of aggravated sexual assault is usually reserved for the most violent of nonconsensual sex acts, where a weapon was used, and either the complainant's life was endangered or they were wounded, maimed, or disfigured. On top of aggravated sexual assault, multiple other charges can also be applied, such as attempted murder, administering a noxious substance, and assault causing bodily harm. Canada is also the only country to successfully prosecute someone on charges of first-degree murder in relation to HIV transmission.

Due to relentless and dedicated activism from legal experts, people living with HIV, and human rights campaigners, there have been recent reforms to Canada's punitive approach. In 2019, the federal government, with jurisdiction solely over the territories, as well as some provinces, has said that it will no longer pursue charges if the person accused of HIV nondisclosure is virally suppressed. In some instances, the use of condoms will also be considered, as well as engagement with public health authorities prior to police intervention.

EXPOSURE CHARGES

In both the United States and Canada, along with criminal cases of nondisclosure, people can be charged in relation to exposure, which is when someone alleges to have been exposed to HIV. Most often this has occurred in cases of spitting, where someone in conflict with the police spits during an arrest. In Canada, the law deems spitting on a police officer as a form of assault. While a less recent phenomenon, there have been several such cases across the country. In 2013 near Gatineau, Quebec, a fifty-year-old HIV-positive Indigenous woman initially called police when her partner had become violent toward her. The woman was arrested in her own home, charged with assault, and sentenced to ten months in prison for allegedly spitting at police officers during an altercation. Even though HIV cannot be transmitted via saliva, the judge presiding over the case convicted the woman, stating that he wanted to send a message to other people living with HIV. The two police officers involved remained HIV negative and took several months of paid leave.

Another example is from Winnipeg, in the province of Manitoba, where a forty-four-year-old HIV-positive Indigenous man was given six and a half years, just short of the maximum sentence of seven years, for allegedly spitting blood into the face of a police officer. The incident took place in 2009, and in 2013, the man was convicted of attempted aggravated assault after a lengthy legal battle. The *Winnipeg Free Press* reported the headline: *Victory seen in case of HIV-positive man who spat at cop.* None of the media reports of the case mentioned why the man's mouth was full of blood while in police custody after his arrest. In custody, police had put a "spit hood" on the man—a contentious piece of netting that's placed over the head to prevent people from spitting. The hoods have been known to cause suffocation and have been banned in some countries. The man was on anti-HIV medication at the time and his viral load indicated as low, meaning that was impossible to transmit, and HIV was not transmitted to the police officer. Police stated in court that the man tried to take the hood off, which the judge used to say the man's actions were premeditated and thus the long sentence. According to reports in the media, the man had spent much of his life either incarcerated or homeless. During his sentencing hearing, he stated, "I would never do anything to harm anyone with [HIV]. In a way I was glad I have it 'cuz the cops won't beat me up no more." It was posted on Facebook by Ted Kerr: "Nowhere in this case is there any mention of the premeditation of the ongoing and genocidal project of settler-colonization, the premeditation that has aimed to systematically destroy the land and culture from which this man is Indigenous."

Such mobilization of fears of infection through impossible means, such as spitting, underlines the discriminatory and often racist ways policing and legal tools have been mobilized against people living with HIV.

PUBLIC HEALTH LEGISLATION

In addition to criminal law, provincial public health laws can also apply to people to regulate HIV. Like other government institutions, such as the police, or the criminal legal system, the work of public health authorities is rooted in a historical legacy of colonization, racism, discrimination, and marginalization. Anyone who does not fit into this idea of the white middle-class public was treated not as people with autonomy and rights but instead as risks to be contained. Furthermore, public health authorities have long treated Black and Indigenous people as experimental testing grounds without their knowledge or consent.[44] This legacy continues today, where institutional racism means government institutions enact racist beliefs into policy, and communities are framed as risks to be managed, not people to be supported.

Sociologist Trevor Hoppe, in writing about the history of HIV criminalization in the United States, specifically in the state of Michigan, uses the term "public health police" to talk about the ways public health authorities "ensure that HIV-positive people behave in a manner officials deem responsible—and how they catch and punish those who do not."[45] Gary Kinsman has noted that throughout history, the *public* in *public health* has been code for white and middle-class, where people living with HIV have not been conceptualized as part of that public.[46]

Across Canada, public health orders are a legal mechanism enabled under provincial public health legislation to manage various communicable disease transmissions. The legal orders are initiated by medical officers of health, who oversee the implementation of public health law in their own jurisdictions, known as a public health unit. A public health unit's jurisdiction can be one entire city or a larger rural area, such as a county. In practice, the initiation of such orders can be arbitrary, founded in morality rather than the science of disease transmission. Depending on the province, the orders can result in legal sanctions, such as fines or short periods of incarceration, if they are not followed. Further, in some provinces, there is no sunset clause for these orders—they never go away and there is no mechanism to lift them. Despite the harsh legal consequences of their actions, medical officers of health are not governed by an oversight body—essentially, they act as judge and jury.

Ontario is Canada's most populous province, which has the highest concentration of people living with HIV in the country and the highest number of criminal prosecutions related to nondisclosure. Historically, the province is known for having a coercive public health legislative framework that can enable powers very similar to that of criminal law. This framework is the Ontario Health Promotion and Protection Act, and under section 22 of the act, which relates to management of communicable diseases, a medical officer of health can issue a written order that may require a person to take or to refrain from taking specific actions—such as requiring condom use and mandated adherence to anti-HIV medications. Such an order does not relate directly to the person having had criminal charges, as the public health and criminal legal systems are separate. There is no general rule for how and when such orders work in concert with criminal laws, but public health law and criminal law often do intersect, and public health orders can be used against people in a criminal law context.

The orders are often delivered in person by a public health nurse, who can also provide a form of counseling around the contents of the order, such as HIV disclosure, condom use, or anti-HIV medication adherence. Orders can be enforced with a $5,000 a day fine for failure to comply or may lead to the realm of criminal sanction if they are not followed. A person who receives such an order has fifteen days to request a hearing at the Health Protection Appeal Board for contestation if they disagree with the order and want to defend themselves. For example, a person will likely be subject to a public health order before any formal criminal charge is applied. A criminal charge coupled with a public health order in a person's past can then increase the intensity of the criminal law's application, or institutions' understanding of a person as an increased risk to the public.

Public health does not operate in a silo. The blurring of the boundaries between the institutional domains of public health and the criminal legal system, or with other authorities, has the potential to produce combined forms of coercion, surveillance, and control. One example is from British Columbia, where, in June 2019, in what was noted as an "unprecedented" intervention, public health authorities in British Columbia collaborated with the Vancouver police to conduct a widely publicized manhunt. The police released the photograph, name, and description of a man who allegedly violated conditions under the provincial Public Health Act for not adhering to his HIV medication regime. He was feared to be virally unsuppressed and therefore infectious.

Another example is from 2018, when a trans woman sex worker living with HIV was identified widely in a police press release in the Canadian prairies as being virally infectious. The press release stated she was "considered to have a high HIV viral load and has not sought treatment for years" and that she was being charged with aggravated sexual assault after a dispute with one of her clients. There have also been a number of instances where public health authorities have worked with children's aid officials to apprehend children from HIV-positive mothers due to breastfeeding. These cases have primarily figured around Black women who are newcomers from Africa or the Caribbean.

Repurposing private health information for police enforcement and investigations underscores how people living with HIV are subject to combined forms of policing and public health measures. This context can result in invasive forms of surveillance, regulation, and control that are focused on monitoring sensitive health information and sexual practices instead of providing support or creating environments of care.

Personhood and the Case of Lizzie Cyr

A central argument I propose in this book is that criminalization is intimately linked to personhood. Legal violence is the way in which the personhood of criminalized people is undone. As a way forward, I appeal for new conceptions of belonging that exist outside of current notions of liberal personhood. To examine this argument, I take a moment to look back in history. Criminalizing people with communicable diseases is not a new phenomenon. HIV criminalization is not some blip or backfiring of the criminal legal system. Nor is Canada's approach to criminalizing people with a disease an issue that emerged solely during the HIV and AIDS epidemic. Criminalizing people with communicable diseases has been part of the Canadian and American criminal legal and public health systems since their inception. To better understand how we got here, it is useful to look to the past. Doing so can help to understand the historical constitution of conceptions of illegality and criminality—including how, over the course of history, people with certain stigmatized diseases came to be understood as threats to be contained and risks to be managed to protect the health of the public. Historian Scott Stern has outlined how in the United States, stemming from the Victorian era, there was a decades-long strategy to imprison "promiscuous" women to control communicable disease and enforce moral purity.[47] A similar campaign existed in Canada. Long before the HIV epidemic, the Dominion of Canada was wrestling for stability as a newly formed settler society and a colony of the United Kingdom. Following the passage of the Constitution Act in 1867, Canada's single federal Criminal Code—which is administered provincially—took force in 1893. By the turn of the century, the country had been hit hard by a series of epidemics. The country had lost approximately 50,000 people during the influenza epidemic and another 50,000 to tuberculosis. The dominion had the highest infant mortality rate in the newly industrialized world. For settler colonies such as Canada, the health and security of the population were equated with the success of the colonial project and of the nation itself. With the rise of new diagnostics, the scope and scale of sexually transmitted infection rates came into view. By 1916, the Canadian army had documented 66,083 cases of what were known as venereal diseases at the time—a catch-all term that included syphilis, gonorrhea, and herpes. The following year, Toronto General Hospital, the main hospital in Canada's largest city, documented a rate of venereal disease of 13 percent among its patients.[48]

In the early 1900s, the project of public health was still a recent invention and became an integral part of establishing settler society. Building public health infrastructure such as clinics and treatment facilities was part of the function of colonization. But there was much fear and stigma surrounding venereal diseases, which were associated with vice, social impurity, and lifestyles that ran counter to settler, middle-class, white ideals. Due to stigma associated with venereal diseases, treatment was not provided in existing hospitals. Instead, there was a strong reliance on criminal legal infrastructure—courts and jails—to handle health-related issues of moral concern. This reliance led to an early blurring of lines between care and control, between coercive public health measures and punishment. In his sociological account of the historical development of laws criminalizing HIV in the United States, Trevor Hoppe asked the question, "When and how does coercion turn punitive in public health practice?"[49] This question is key to continually ask when examining the historical development laws criminalizing issues of morality and stigma, such as venereal diseases.

The blurring of treatment with punishment particularly impacted women. In this context, women from the upper classes were often leaders in the campaigns for the criminalization of poor, Indigenous, and nonwhite immigrant women. This movement came to be known as the moral reform movement. Moral reformers led the charge to address the health and social challenges of the new settler state of Canada, aiming to promote forms of white middle-class values and purity through promoting public health and criminalizing those they saw as threats to their project.

"Lizzie Cyr, I sentence you to six months hard labour"

One such criminalized woman was Lizzie Cyr. In 1917, Cyr, a Métis woman from Calgary, Alberta, was charged with vagrancy. Métis refers to a collective of ethnic identities and cultures resulting from unions between Indigenous and European people in the settler colony of Canada. One of Cyr's clients complained to the police that he had paid for sex with Cyr, and she had transmitted gonorrhea to him. The police subsequently arrested her in her own home, which was odd due to the vagrancy charge. Given that the legal definition of a vagrant was someone without a stable place of residence, "lodging in a barn or outhouse."[50] However, the criminal charge of vagrancy was vague and multipurpose, which enabled it to be mobilized easily to regulate sex work and sexually transmitted infections.

In the Criminal Code at the time, vagrancy was defined as "a loose, idle, or disorderly person or vagrant [without] any visible means of subsistence."[51] As noted by historian David Bright, vagrancy in early Calgary was a "crime of status rather than a crime of action."[52] Vagrancy—repealed from the Criminal Code as a criminal act in 1972—is no longer the crime of social significance that it was at the time. when it was conflated poverty, sex work, and racialization with criminality.

Cyr's vagrancy case came to a women's court overseen by the police magistrate Alice Jamieson. Moral reformer Emily Murphy made history as the first woman to become a magistrate in the British Commonwealth. Following Murphy, Jamieson was the second woman to take such a role. Together,

FIG. 1.7. The case of Lizzie Cyr

Murphy and Jaimeson presided over the women's court, a court for low-level offenses to be heard. Cyr's lawyer, J. McKinley Cameron, was known to take on pro bono cases of socially disadvantaged groups in society, including Chinese migrant workers, sex workers, miners, and gamblers.

FIG. 1.8. The case of Lizzie Cyr continued

Cameron made a series of arguments challenging Cyr's charge. First, Cameron stated that Cyr could not be considered a vagrant, as the law only applied to men, since the vagrancy provision in the Criminal Code used only the pronoun "him." The second argument was that the presiding judge, Jamieson, was a woman, and women were not qualified to hold judicial office because they were not considered persons under the law. (This second line of defense was used by many of the defendants who came before the courts of the new women police magistrates.) Cameron stated that the vagrancy provision was too vague and did not specify anything related to sex work. Finally, Cameron also believed that Cyr's client was equally responsible for the infection and that the burden should not rest on Cyr alone. To Cyr's accuser, Cameron noted in court, "It takes two to have sexual intercourse. Are you a decent man?"[53]

The issue of women not being legally recognized in the Criminal Code was one that the moral reform movement of women was aware of and had been working to remedy. After her appointment to her position as police magistrate, Emily Murphy began lobbying the Alberta attorney general to reform the Criminal Code so that women practicing sex work could be explicitly charged with vagrancy. She argued that the word "herself" could be added to the provision, as she was eager to be able to adequately criminalize the problem she regarded as a social scourge inhibiting a pure settler state.[54]

Nevertheless, Jamieson disagreed with all of Cameron's defense arguments—and paid little attention to the fact that the vagrancy provision as stated may not have been applicable to women. She stated in court, "Lizzie Cyr, I sentence you to six months hard labour at MacLeod."[55] This was the maximum sentence available in the Criminal Code for the offence of vagrancy. Cyr was sent to the MacLeod Common Gaol. It was run by the colonial police force, the Northwest Mounted Police, which later became the Royal Canadian Mounted Police (RCMP) and was well known for its poor conditions, disease outbreaks, and as a site of capital punishment. The prison was also used as a quasi-lock hospital to house women who had sexually transmitted diseases. These lock hospitals also served as a solution to the stigma around treating venereal diseases in regular hospitals. A lock hospital was a hybrid institution providing both care and control, confined women were not free to leave until they were cured or died of the treatments. Before the advent of penicillin, treatment for venereal disease was long and painful, with a limited success rate and many deaths. It could take up to five years to be clear of the infection, and it involved three injections of arsenic a week, called arsenicals, as well as the topical application of mercury. The mercury treatment cleared the skin, but it did not kill the underlying ailment. The combination treatment was intense, and many would die of shock immediately, while others died slowly of arsenic and mercury poisoning. The sites of injection were excruciatingly painful and caused exhaustion and general malaise as the body coped with being slowly and methodically poisoned.

At the time, the work of incarcerating women like Cyr was considered a benevolent endeavor to support the success of settler society. When incarcerating women like Cyr, the magistrates would use an Information and Complaint form, the document used to detail a criminal offense against the Criminal Code with which a person was charged. Emily Murphy, in some instances, was known to cross out the verb "did" with an "x" and would instead write, "was infected with venereal disease."[56] This meant, for a time, women were being incarcerated solely for having a sexually transmitted infection; criminality and venereal disease became one and the same.

Other women magistrates and moral reformers were known to keep in correspondence with women who had been incarcerated and would send them fabric for quilting projects. In keeping with the project of moral reform, the incarcerated women were understood as inferior but still in need of care and sympathy while being kept from public view. The control of Indigenous women's bodies was central to the project of colonization. Several provinces, led by Alberta, also enacted eugenics laws encouraging the forced and coerced sterilization of Indigenous women, labeling them "feebleminded" and in need of state control to ensure the purity of the population.[57]

Cyr's lawyer, Cameron, continued to push her case and appealed Jamieson's decision. But the higher court's response to whether women were eligible to hold office was lukewarm. Facing an onslaught of resistance to women's new judicial authority, Emily Murphy mobilized to remedy the situation. Emily Murphy worked alongside four other prominent middle-class activists—Henrietta Muir Edwards, Nellie McClung, Louise Crummy McKinney, and Irene Parlby—who agreed with Cyr's prosecution. Together they later became known as "the Famous Five." They wanted to instrumentalize Cyr's case to win the right for women in Canada to be recognized as legal persons under the law. Such a right would also allow women to hold judicial office. In maintaining judicial positions, they sought to use the criminal law to incarcerate sex workers, Indigenous women, and women with venereal disease as part of the project of moral reform in the dominion. Cyr's case was used to help argue for this cause.

Alberta's highest court agreed with the group, legally reaffirming Alice Jamieson as a judge overseeing the women's court on November 26, 1917.[58] The decision made Alberta the first province to recognize this right for women. Historian David Bright, reflecting on the decision of the Alberta court in his article "The Other Woman: Lizzie Cyr and the Origins of the 'Persons Case,'" noted, "The Alberta court was not simply affirming an abstract principle when it ruled in favour of Alice Jamieson in 1917, but instead was upholding the concrete conviction of a woman accused of prostitution. By doing so, the legal system not only confirmed the right of Jamieson to hold high public office, but—and just as importantly—it reinforced the social assumptions and prejudices on which she had based her conviction of Cyr in the first place."[59]

However, the Alberta victory did not extend far enough for the group of moral reformers. The law was not consistent across Canada, so the women took their argument to the Supreme Court of Canada, which, on April 24, 1928, ruled against the Famous Five, underlining that women were still not legal persons who could preside over a court or hold other forms of official government office. As Canada was still under the dominion of the United Kingdom, there was still one higher authority to which they could attempt their argument: the British Privy Council. The Famous Five appealed, and the Privy Council overruled the Supreme Court's decision on October 18, 1929. The decision deemed women in Canada were indeed legal persons.

The moral reform project of incarcerating women with venereal disease had not abated disease transmissions. Due to the efforts of Murphy and the moral reformers, the prison population among women tripled across Alberta. Murphy alone incarcerated seventy-five women who were documented as having venereal diseases in 1921 and sixty-six cases in 1922.[60] The punitive approach had not worked to control disease but legitimized the regulation of diseases of vice with enforcement and punishment. (The only thing that eventually abated the epidemics of sexually transmitted infections was the advent of penicillin, which did not reach widespread use in Canada until 1943.)

So, while Lizzie Cyr still did six months of hard labor, women with access to wealth and status were able to continue to prosecute other women such as Cyr. The liberal notion of personhood in law, as it is still understood today in Canada, rests on the back of Cyr, who was prosecuted for vagrancy as a sex worker, and Métis woman, with a venereal disease. In efforts of settler moral reformers to expand the definition of legal personhood for themselves, Murphy and the others fought to deliberately exclude and criminalize others, such as women like Cyr. The colonial liberal legal architecture of personhood in Canadian society is thus constituted in part through the criminalization of sex work, people of color, and people with sexually transmitted infections.

Lizzie Cyr's case shows how people with communicable diseases—specifically those related to sex and sexuality—have historically been subject to coercive and punitive forms of legal violence. With the gendered linking of criminality and infection, it was not a specific moral wrong that rendered a woman a criminal but, rather, who she was, the color of her skin, or the infection she had within her body that turned her into a risk to the respectable white settler public. The criminal legal system and public health institutions have always been intertwined when it comes to developing responses to disease control. It also becomes apparent how constituting criminality relies on the deconstitution of legal personhood. Cyr lost her liberty, privacy, and ability to support herself, as well as her access to safety and security. It is not known what became of Cyr, and the only reason we know of her now is because she became engaged with the criminal legal system.

As with the case of Cyr and others who later came to be charged in relation to HIV-related crimes, mobilizing histories helps us understand processes of criminalization to interrogate and denaturalize the process, to see how things came to be as they are today.

Research as Bearing Witness

Examining criminalization as a form of violence, for me, means there is an ethical imperative to take a political stance in this work, one that carries with it the ethical duties of an active subject beyond the role of mere observer. I explain taking a political stance through the idea of bearing witness. Undertaking this project, I understood my role as a researcher to be one of bearing witness to the avoidable suffering of criminalized people. This moves my role beyond someone who merely documents the harms to criminalization for academic study. Bearing witness, rather, acknowledges my role to take care in how I handle the complexity of the information I collected and to take what I learned forward in the form of testimony supporting actions calling for change.

For my research, I mobilized a critical ethnographic approach, or a *criminology of the criminalized*, one focused from the perspectives of criminalized people. My research is aligned with the historical trajectory of critical social science research, where attention is paid to systems of oppression and the resulting suffering of people.[61] The aim of this approach is to develop knowledge that contends with avoidable forms of suffering that results from criminalization, which in turn can support efforts calling for emancipation and social change. Albeit with a caveat: one research project can only do so much. I have grown tired of the lofty emancipatory promises that some researchers throw around. So, while I have emancipatory activist objectives, I understand the limits of what is possible within the bounds of academic research.

This qualitative research project was also grounded in the tradition of institutional ethnography, the alternative feminist form of sociological inquiry developed by Dorothy Smith.[62] Methods from institutional ethnography enable social research to be developed from the perspective of those who experience the problem at hand. This methodology is deeply epistemologically aligned to center the experiences of criminalized people, as institutional ethnographic research takes place from the location of the experience of social actors as they see and understand the world around them. This means that the frame of analysis for my work is situated in the daily lived experiences of criminalized people. With institutional ethnography, from the ground up, the researcher can then look to the ways in which people's daily lives are socially organized, constrained, regulated, and controlled by extralocal forces. For the project of denaturalizing violence—I mobilize institutional ethnography to examine the daily violence in criminalized people's lives, from their own perspective. This analysis views the daily violence of criminalization not just understanding it as random acts, instead linking those forms of violence to a complex system of institutions.

Institutional ethnography practitioners develop knowledge that can help to decenter the dominant ways of knowing, thinking about, documenting, and remembering people.[63] In this case, I track the discourses of a diverse array of institutions engaged with socially organizing public health and criminal legal responses to HIV to help understand how they shape people's daily lives. Central to this approach is exploring the disjuncture between people's lived experiences and how they come to be known institutionally.

My approach to research as bearing witness is aligned with calls from bell hooks, who developed knowledge so as to talk back to systems of violence and oppression from a stance of equal authority and power,[64] and Audra Simpson, who's scholarship is an act of refusal to accept the carceral logics of the settler state.[65] Also, this work follows the trajectory of qualitative insight into the lives of people living with HIV, such as Celeste Watkins-Hayes's work examining intersecting forms of stigma that circumscribe the lives of women living with HIV in America. Watkins-Hayes mobilizes a "sociology of the transformative project" and, using qualitative research, seeks to examine how women living with HIV move from the viewpoint of "dying from" to "living with" the virus.[66] Like Watkins-Hayes, I do not wish to make any didactic allusions to the research process as emancipatory. But, in the context of critical research attuned to suffering, it is important to engage the notion of bearing witness to bring an ethical dimension into this work—to acknowledge the social justice issues at hand and the potential of research to serve a broader social purpose.

THE INTERVIEWS

The stories in this book are an outcome of twenty-seven in-depth qualitative interviews I conducted with sixteen people (four cis women, one trans woman, and eleven cis men) across five provinces in Canada, along with archival research. The youngest person I interviewed was in their mid-teens at the time of the charges. The oldest was in their mid-fifties at the time of the charges. Some people had been charged only a few months after testing HIV positive, while others had known their HIV-positive status for several years.

The earliest charges were around the year 2000, and the most recent charges were from 2015. Of the sixteen people interviewed, three had been threatened with criminal charges by police, while thirteen had been formally criminally charged, all with aggravated sexual assault. Some faced multiple other charges, including attempted murder, all related to alleged HIV nondisclosure. In only one of the cases was HIV transmission alleged to have taken place.

People participated in this project because they wanted me and others to bear witness to what happened to them as a form of healing and justice. Over the course of two years, I spent time with each person, attending appointments with them, sharing meals, going for walks, and hanging out with them in their homes. We talked about their lives and their aspirations, as well as the impacts of criminalization. A focus of our discussions was on the material outcomes of being institutionally marked as a "criminal" and a "risk to public safety." The interviews consisted of detailed questions about people's experiences from the time they found out they had been criminally charged (or were threatened with charges), as well as—if applicable—their arrest, court proceedings, sentencing, incarceration, release, and lives after their sentencing.

In many cases, when I interviewed people, I was the first person to whom they spoke about their experiences of criminalization. The people I interviewed were only able to tell me what they knew about their experience. Prior to being criminalized, people already lacked privacy in their daily lives due to various forms of social marginalization. Some people were in transition houses, under curfew, or lived in shelters. Because of lack of access to privacy and that people had nowhere else to speak to me honestly about their lives, many of the interviews were conducted in the coffee and donut shop Tim Hortons. We, of course, ensured that no one overheard our discussions.

For many, the experiences they described were traumatizing and their memory was one of shock, shame, and depression. Specific details and facts were sometimes a challenge. Some did not know the full name of the charges against them or have a full understanding of the legal proceedings and procedures that took place in their cases. I acted as a witness to their memory, as someone they could speak to about what had been done to them. While my approach was to trust people as experts in their own experience, in some cases, when technical details were required, I went to other sources to verify accuracy.

Part of my process of recruiting people to speak with me was identifying my HIV-positive status. Generally, people assumed that we had some sort of common understanding. As people living with the virus, that was not the case, and my HIV-positive status, along with being a white gay man only went so far to bridging the differences.

Along with spending time, I often conducted more than one interview with people. The content of the second interview provided greater insight, allowing people to open up to me in greater detail so I could ask if I correctly understood and interpreted their experiences. In addition, the second interview proved extremely effective for building and establishing both trust and rapport. During the second interview, I was invited into people's homes, asked to share meals, and introduced to people's family members. In one instance, someone told me that they had lied to me during the first interview about some minor details of their incarceration but, during the second interview, wanted me to know the truth and corrected the lie. Furthermore, during the second interview, people also told me about some of the more sensitive aspects of their experiences, including moments of extreme violence they faced. Some people noted that they felt more comfortable having previously met with me before discussing in detail the most difficult aspects of their experiences.

OBJECTIFICATION, OR OTHER PEOPLE ARE REAL

As a researcher, the notion of bearing witness asserts my role as an active observer with ethical obligations. One starting point for this approach is to consider what Sarah Schulman underlined to me continually during a creative writing seminar that I took with her in the summer of 2018: that "other people are real." In the context of my research, I take the statement that other people are real to mean that what I produce must bring a complex subjectivity, autonomy, depth, and agency to the people who shared their stories with me. With this sentiment, people are regarded as active agents, not solely subjects of research.

But research is also the process of creating a knowledge product—this book itself—that could potentially objectify the very subjects experiencing criminalization. Could a problem emerge here related to exploitation, voyeurism, and objectification? Could focusing on the violence of criminalization result in imagining people only as subjects of violence? Philosopher Susan Sontag addresses this problem while asking a series of ethical questions regarding visual eyewitness testimony of suffering in her book *Regarding the Pain of Others*. Sontag asks if bearing witness when viewing photography represents a form of exploitation if one is external to the experiences of suffering and violence.[67] Sontag notes that photographic eyewitness accounts of war, atrocities, and state violence can render experiences of suffering into something that can be possessed, where the photographs become objects, which can act to objectify their subjects and turn them into commodities.

Sontag further notes that there should be no assumption of a universal "we" when looking at images of violence, or that the viewers of such photographs would hold the same values, understandings, or critiques of violence. With her analysis, Sontag asks what purpose such images serve. Do pictures of suffering and violence simply make us feel bad? Do they immobilize and desensitize us? Does viewing them make us better people? Or can viewing them create an initial spark to mobilize us into action? Sontag argues that we should not take for granted any assumption about the function of images of suffering and violence. Rather, the way in which these images are presented and engaged with can help frame our ethical engagement with them.

Finally, Sontag asks, "What does it mean to protest suffering, as distinct from acknowledging it?" This question creates an ethical role for the observer who bears witness to the suffering of people. I apply Sontag's questions about photographs to the outcomes of research on criminalization. Sontag's questions are vital for a project of research aimed at denaturalizing violence. When the knowledge we seek to capture as researchers relates to the trauma, pain, and suffering of people, a delicate balance exists between exploitation and developing knowledge to support changing the conditions that produced that violence in the first place.

ON WRITING ABOUT VIOLENCE

Many of the experiences I heard and described are graphic, shocking, and difficult to comprehend. After collecting the stories that comprise this book, it took me a long time to present my research findings without crying. Despite my investment in the issue as an activist and someone living with HIV, I wanted to ensure that any presentation of stories did not become about me as the researcher. In other words, I needed to *get a grip* and figure out how to write about and speak about these stories with respect and grace, but not in a way that detracted from my objectives. The experiences needed to stand outside of me on their own. To do so, I channeled the intention of people who spoke with me—their drive and passion to seek justice. They propped me up and propelled me forward to amplify what had been shared, so others could also hear and understand.

Throughout the writing phase of this project, I continually referred to the ethical questions posed by Sontag while elaborating the notion of bearing witness. In writing about the experiences of violence faced by the people I interviewed, these questions oriented my use of language and the descriptions that emerged. These considerations were twofold: first, I wanted to ensure justice was done to the stories that people entrusted to me, and second, I wanted to avoid alienating, overwhelming, or immobilizing the reader. I thus aimed to avoid sensationalistic or political language and remained conscious to avoid editorializing or making judgments, instead allowing the experiences to stand for themselves. I often reflected, while constructing a narrative from the interview transcripts, on whether this research was exploitative. That is, where was the line between explaining what happened to people and being gratuitous? Ensuring that the language I used and descriptions I constructed were explained as plainly as possible, required a reflective negotiation throughout the writing process.

A NOTE ON PRIVACY

Privacy is crucial when it comes to research on issues of criminality. Without a promise of confidentiality, my research would not have been possible, as no one would have spoken to me. I received ethics clearance from Concordia University, where I was doing my doctoral research. The ethics process hinged on guarantees of confidentiality. Privacy is of vital importance for people who have had their trust broken many times, such as repeatedly having their HIV status and charges outed by police and media, or their privacy breached by their doctors and nurses. Throughout this book, I avoid the unnecessary reproduction of criminalized people's names without their consent. This means I use pseudonyms when discussing the experiences of living people who have been criminalized. This is the case when discussing the experiences of people interviewed for this project, and when discussing the experiences of living people whom I examined from archival or media research.

When shifting the analytical framework to the experiences of people who have lived through criminalization, some issues that typically remain unquestioned when writing about criminality arise. For example, it is common when examining legal cases in Canada to use individuals' last names to refer to a precedent or to well-known cases. Using an individual's last name when discussing a criminal case goes unchallenged, since people with histories of criminalization are denied autonomy over their own life history in multiple ways. This means, merely discussing the case means we are repeatedly disclosing the person's HIV status and criminal charges. And while this information may already be in the public sphere, it can cause ongoing harm.

However, once you speak directly with the people whose names are attached to these criminal legal cases and whose names can then be reproduced repeatedly, it emerges that identifying a case by someone's name can be an unjust practice. Doing so repeatedly discloses someone's HIV-positive status and criminal charges without their consent.

It marks them as criminals for life, beyond them having served time. Understanding how these small practices result in an injustice can help us view things from the perspectives of those who have lived through criminalization.

WHO IS MISSING?

There are many people's accounts missing from this book. People who had migrated to Canada and had then been deported after being prosecuted. People who died while incarcerated. People who are still incarcerated. Over the course of my field research, I was in touch with many different people, but for a range of reasons, including incarceration, deportation, lack of interest, concerns about stigma, discrimination, and reprisals, or further criminal charges, as well as just wanting to move past their experience, some did not engage in interviews. Some people were in the process of defending their case, and their lawyers decided they should not participate (although being in an ongoing trial did not automatically exclude someone, and I did also speak to several people who were in the middle of court proceedings).

I was not able to interview people who are currently incarcerated, but I interviewed many people with histories of incarceration. In Canada, it is notoriously difficult to interview prisoners, and interview questions need to be vetted by prison authorities to ensure the research outcomes are not critical of prison institutions. This makes it near impossible to get an accurate account of the ongoing experience of incarceration. On top of this, prison officials do not allow interviews with what they call "high-profile offenders." It is an unfortunate fact that many people with HIV-related criminalization cases have been widely sensationalized in the media, meaning that if someone is still incarcerated, it is also near impossible to be allowed to interview them while they are inside due to this rule. I was also concerned about putting incarcerated people at risk, as my interview questions asked people about the conditions of their confinement. Being critical of those conditions while still incarcerated could have put someone in jeopardy with prison officials who are notoriously retributive. It became more feasible to interview people who had served time and were released. Furthermore, deportation is a common outcome of HIV criminalization prosecutions, and many people prosecuted have been racialized migrants from other countries. While I worked to locate people who had been deported, it was untenable. A number of those still facing long sentences or who have been deported are Black men, meaning that a deeper understanding of the racialized dynamics of HIV criminalization is out of view due to intentional obfuscation from corrections authorities and from harmful practices of border control.

What Follows

In the following chapter of this book, I discuss the process of criminalization, that of turning complex experiences into cases to be managed, rendering people into subjects of legal violence. I discuss the ways in which a wide range of information and institutions come to intersect and produce criminalization, which reaches beyond the bounds of the criminal legal system and is dispersed throughout all aspects of criminalized people's lives. I examine, in detail, the various forms of violence faced by criminalized people, when their personhood is taken away from them, and how criminalization is used to justify the use of legal and extralegal violence toward them. With this analysis, I hope to contribute to critiques challenging the administration of punishment in society, to bear witness and call for action, and to form the political basis of a life worth living—one flourishing—for people who have been subject to criminalization in relation HIV. My hope it to put into question settler-colonial liberal criminal legal regimes, which have produced the contemporary concept of personhood, and the limited conception of justice that seeks to enact violence as a remedy to social problems. There is a broad and diverse global movement of people living with HIV, activists, legal experts, politicians, and academics working to change the ways HIV is criminalized and calling for decriminalization. This is a movement I am actively part of and a movement that has deeply informed the development of my research. In the final chapter, I document movements of resistance to criminalization, working in, against, and beyond the system.

~ 2 ~

The Making of a Case

In 1987, activist and researcher George Smith—a founding member of the Toronto-based AIDS ACTION NOW!—wrote in the queer Canadian periodical *Rites*, "It looks as though the police in Toronto will continue to shape the politics of AIDS in the city for some time to come."[1] Smith was referring to an incident where Toronto Police Services officers were publicly criticized for the use of excessive force after shooting canisters of tear gas into the home of an unarmed man living with HIV following complaints that he had dementia and was causing disturbances in the neighborhood. The man was detained under mental health legislation. After appeals for mental health experts and HIV support organizations, the police apologized and said they would work to better sensitize officers. But Smith was right:

the teargas incident set the stage for the policing of people living with HIV for years to come.

In 1988, in Quebec City, a woman working as a sex worker was banned from part of the city where she was known to work. She was banned because she was living with HIV and feared a risk. Authorities mobilized a city ordinance against her. Later, one of her clients complained to police that he believed he contracted HIV from her. She had been ignoring the ordinance, and she was arrested by police. The woman was charged with disobeying the ordinance and incarcerated for five months. The media reported "La prostituée side demeurera en prison,"[2] which roughly translates to "the prostitute with AIDS will remain in prison."

Criminal law was not mobilized in the above cases. However, due to social panic surrounding AIDS, criminal charges were soon to come. In 1989, one of the earliest known cases of HIV-related criminal charges was a twenty-four-year-old man, whom I will refer to with the pseudonym Sam, from Calgary, Alberta. Sam was living with a new HIV diagnosis. Initially, according to media reports, he was charged with aggravated assault and attempting to cause bodily harm. But those charges were dropped when two women to whom he was accused of transmitting HIV refused to testify against him. According to media reports, both women Sam had had sex with had tested positive for HIV, but it was also reported that they had forgiven Sam. He pled guilty to the charge of being a common nuisance and was sentenced to one year of imprisonment and three years of probation.

In Canada, prosecutors represent the people, but also still the British monarchy, and are therefore known as Crown prosecutors. In Sam's case, the Crown prosecutor stated that he likely had hundreds of potential "victims."[3] Even if the two women had forgiven Sam, charges would still move forward in the interest if the public. Sam went to the media, intending to clear his name, stating that there were only ten people likely at risk, many of whom he had already disclosed his HIV-positive status to prior to sex. He stated in court that the reason he originally chose not to disclose his HIV status to the two women in question was due to his own denial. He stated that he wanted to live a normal life. Also, based on his understanding, he was healthy because he was asymptomatic.

Sam's appeals for understanding did not fly with the court. At the trial, provincial court Judge Robert Dinkel noted, "I am satisfied the accused's actions were promiscuous and that it constitutes endangering the safety of the public, the accused's chances of reform are, in my view, small."[4] Judge Dinkel also condemned the two women for not coming forward to testify against Sam. Media outlets reported on Sam's bisexuality and ran headlines labeling him an "AIDS spreader."

The next year, on a different case focused on a sex worker, the medical officer of health in Victoria, British Columbia, called for a wider use of criminal sanctions. The local media ran an article, stating "Health Laws Too Weak to Stop AIDS Hooker," noting that the medical officer of health wanted tougher sanctions to incapacitate a sex worker living with HIV, and appealed to Crown prosecutors to use criminal laws. In the end, the woman in question was banned completely from the town using a city ordinance.

In 1991, another case emerged. A twenty-year-old woman was arrested in Nanaimo, British Columbia, for allegedly having condomless sex with two men without first disclosing she was HIV positive. At the time, media reported that this was the third case in Canada of police targeting someone due to the alleged nondisclosure of their HIV-positive status and the first case targeting a woman. The woman, whom I refer to with the pseudonym Anna, was arrested by RCMP Inspector Dennis Brown, who later addressed the media, stating that charges of aggravated sexual assault would be applied.

The origins of the RCMP, Canada's national police force, underscore the ongoing legacy of colonization facing the country. As the coercive arm of colonial policy, the North West Mounted Police (predecessor to the RCMP) were instrumental in displacing and containing Indigenous peoples in the West to open the land for settlement, resource extraction, and Canadian expansion. The institutional origins of policing in Canada were informed by a colonial civilizing mission and underwritten with a sense of racial settler superiority that associated Indigenous peoples with crime, deviance, and dissent.[5]

Anna's case was the first instance of a Crown prosecutor seeking this charge for alleged nondisclosure. Apparently, no evidence existed that the complainants contracted the virus (and it is also physiologically much more difficult for a woman to transmit the virus during heterosexual intercourse than it is for her to acquire it from someone else).[6,7] The provincial attorney general Colin Gabelmann noted that Anna was carrying a deadly virus and she was under a public health order to not engage in condomless sex, further stating, "What may be new is the laying of an aggravated sexual assault [charge] in this type of case. That may be ground-breaking."[8]

Anna was originally denied bail. However, after a review by a British Columbia Supreme Court judge, she was released on the condition that she stay at a transition house for women, abide by a curfew, report to a probation officer and public health officers, and refrain from having unprotected sex.

Because the case represented a first of its kind and was highly contentious, it generated a wide range of media attention in various local and national newspapers. A coalition of women's groups across Canada spoke out against Anna's charge: "To us it is unconscionable that laws designed to protect women from sexual violence would be used in this manner to jail a woman," said a representative from the AIDS Committee of Ottawa.[9] "The charge of aggravated sexual assault is an insult to any woman who has ever been sexually assaulted," added a representative of the Canadian Association of Sexual Assault Centres. The coalition mobilized some members of parliament from the federal New Democratic Party, and they also put pressure on British Columbia's provincial government.

The head of the local community-based AIDS organization that provided care, education, and support, AIDS Vancouver, also responded publicly that he was concerned Anna was being singled out, noting, "When people are having sex, everybody should assume they (their partners) are HIV-positive. And why are the two men having unprotected sex? It's incumbent on both parties to ensure they're protecting themselves." Working with the direct-action activist group ACT UP Vancouver, both organizations held a public demonstration and started raising money to help finance Anna's legal defense. They were angered that the newspaper *The Province* named Anna in a front-page article. ACT UP Vancouver members held a "die-in" in front of *The Pacific Press* building in response to that newspaper's coverage of the story. ACT UP Vancouver said Anna was being scapegoated and persecuted: "Women do not wear condoms, men do," became a slogan at a rally where ACT UP Vancouver members chalked outlines of their bodies on sidewalks to represent the people who had died from AIDS.

Eventually, the Ministry of Justice decided to drop the charges against Anna. They considered that she had not had appropriate counseling to manage and understand her condition. It was reported that the Crown prosecutor felt the case should be dealt with via provincial public health legislation rather than the federal Criminal Code. A spokesperson for the Ministry of Justice told the press that criminal charges would only apply if a person exhibited a criminal intent to harm others. These initial instances of intervention, where people were turned into cases, were related to morality and stigma concerning mental health, sex work, and sexuality. We only know of the people living with HIV in these histories because people became cases that were dispersed into the public realm. Furthermore, these initial cases help to provide insight into how the criminalization of HIV was negotiated and organized collectively by policing, criminal legal, public health, and media institutions.

Cases

When someone is criminalized due to HIV, or for other reasons, their lived experiences can come to be framed outside of their own understanding. This is the process whereby people become cases. To make a case, public health authorities, police, and courts transform a complex experience into a series of institutional facts that are, in turn, mobilized to justify certain legal outcomes. Information from authorities comes to create formal knowledge of the situation, which constitutes a case. Through being transformed into cases, people's lived experiences are rendered into an abstraction of their actual experience. At the same time, there is resistance to the construction of cases, where the people involved or interested parties can counter official ways of knowing.

In this chapter, I present the experiences of three people whom I have interviewed: Shaun, Lenore, and Cynthia. Each person describes the nascent stages of their engagement with policing and public health institutions and recalls how they came to understand that they were being criminally charged in relation to HIV nondisclosure. The criminal legal system forces nuanced situations—circumstances that involve people's silence, fear, actual disclosure, or, in some cases, inability to address their own HIV status—into the dichotomous narrative of victim/perpetrator. Becoming a case stands as the institutional entry point that enables the social and systemic processes required to criminalize individuals.

There's no single way whereby a person becomes a case. Some individuals learn that they have become a case when they engage with the police as their first point of institutional contact. That is, they may be called upon to appear at a local police station, be arrested in public seemingly out of the blue, or turn themselves in after being notified of a warrant for their arrest.

For others, the first point of institutional engagement occurs with public health officials. For example, they may receive a public health order or meet with a public health official after they test positive for HIV.

Regardless of how it occurs, becoming a case is a relational process, which—in the context of HIV criminalization—relies on both formal institutional processes and social processes that intersect with policing, the criminal legal system, public health institutions, and the media.

Finally, what I mean by being turned into a case should not be confused with the specific acts of wrongdoing or harm that the people in question have allegedly committed. Instead, a person becomes a case when they interact with, and have their experiences recorded by, authoritative institutions. It must be noted that the project of this book is not one of determining or attributing wrongdoing or blame. Rather, I share these stories to help consider what happens to people who are turned into cases as a means of enabling criminalization. By considering the experiences of criminalized people from their own perspectives, my aim is to disarticulate people from the criminal legal and public health narratives of victim/perpetrator and risk and threat. This approach allows us to examine the nuance and complexity that is so often stripped from the public and institutional understanding of such experiences.

Dichotomization, Legal Facts, and Disjuncture

I present three points of interest that provide insight into the processes of the making of a case for criminalization: the dichotomization of criminalized people's experiences into institutional categories of victim/perpetrator, the organization of experiences into a series of legal facts necessary to produce a legal outcome, and the disjuncture between the experiences of criminalized people and institutional ways of knowing. Once people are institutionally framed as cases, people begin to lose autonomy over their own experiences, this is the entryway into the deconstitution of personhood.

SHAUN

It was spring 2016 and tulips were in full bloom. The sun was shining through the window of the light rail I was traveling on and felt hot on my face as I made my way across town. I was here in the suburbs of a large Canadian city to meet Shaun, a young man in his late twenties. I had seen Shaun's face many times, since his case had been widely publicized in the media at the time of his arrest, his mugshot reproduced in the media over and over. We had talked on the phone once before to arrange the logistics of our meeting, so this was the first time we met in person.

When I arrived at his apartment, he offered me a coffee and introduced me to his dog, a large, friendly Doberman Pinscher. Shaun lived in a high-rise building where most tenants were low income and worked in a factory north of his place. He had moved to Canada five years prior from the Caribbean Island of Saint Vincent to go to college. He was a relaxed guy with a warm smile. I sat down on his couch and explained more about my project to him, and then I turned on my digital recorder.

Shaun learned that he was HIV positive two years after he moved to Canada. "I started getting sick with fevers and long colds," he said. "It was getting serious, so I booked a checkup with a doctor." "The doctor said I was undetectable. I was not a high risk," Shaun told me. He shared the news with his partner, a woman around his own age. They had been dating for about six months. Being undetectable meant Shaun could not transmit HIV and they had always used condoms when they had sex.

But his partner was still worried about her own health when Shaun disclosed his status, so he took her to meet a doctor and speak to the public health authorities. At the clinic, one of the health care professionals told Shaun and his girlfriend that it was against the law for an HIV-positive person to have sex with someone without telling them their status first. His partner took an HIV test, which came back negative. Shaun told me they both felt relieved.

Shaun and his partner stayed in their relationship, and the couple moved into an apartment together. After Shaun found out his status, he hoped to move on from drinking and

FIG. 2.1. Shaun's story part 1

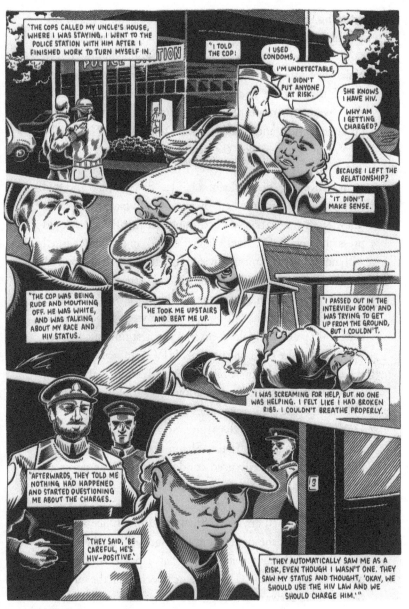

FIG. 2.2. Shaun's story part 2

partying. Shaun wanted to focus on other things; his priorities had changed. "I couldn't keep up with my partner," he said. "I needed things to slow down. I stopped going out to clubs. We talked and she said she'd change her lifestyle, too. I thought we had worked it out, but down the road there were still more problems." Their relationship took a downward turn and Shaun decided to break it off.

When Shaun ended the relationship, things got worse, and it was more hostile between them. He moved out and went to live with his uncle for a while. "She got mad and told me, 'You can't leave me here by myself. You have to pay.' She knew from our earlier visit to public health that she could press charges. A few weeks later I ended up getting charged with nondisclosure and aggravated sexual assault. Two counts."

Shaun explained to me that his ex-partner did not actually want to press charges—she was just upset with him that their relationship was falling apart. She went to police after the breakup and had told them that the first time she had sex with Shaun, she did not know his HIV status. She said that she only found out about his HIV-positive status afterward, and then she continued in a relationship with him. What she did not tell the police was that Shaun was unaware of his HIV-positive status at that time, and as soon as he found out, he also told her. Again, Shaun was undetectable, and they had also regularly used condoms. There was never an allegation that HIV was transmitted. "They asked her if she even wanted to press charges and she was, like, 'no' but, you know, it happened anyhow," Shaun told me. Once a case is in the hands of the police, and it is agreed that the Crown prosecutor will move it forward, what happens is no longer up to the complainant. From the perspective of the authorities, moving forward with aggravated sexual assault charges was perceived as serving the public's interest.

The police called his uncle's house, where Shaun was staying. Shaun told me he was scared, and he went to the police station immediately, with his uncle by his side, to turn himself in and figure out what was going on. "It didn't make sense. I told the cop, 'I used condoms, I was undetectable, I didn't put anyone at risk. She knew I had HIV,'" said Shaun. "'Why am I getting charged? Because I left the relationship?' The cop was being rude and mouthing off, he was white, and was talking about my race, being Black, and my HIV."

The police officer took Shaun upstairs to an interview room. Shaun told me the police officer then beat him up brutally and left him on the floor. "I passed out in the interview room and was trying to get up from the ground, but I couldn't. I was screaming for help, but no one was helping. I felt like I had broken ribs, and I couldn't breathe properly," he said. About an hour later, what felt like ages to Shaun, police officers took him to another room. They told Shaun nothing had happened and started questioning him. When Shaun challenged them about the physical assault, the officers denied anything had happened. He was still holding his ribs in pain.

Sitting across from me in a chair, Shaun explained that the police were unaware of the risks associated with HIV. The officers did not understand that having an undetectable viral load meant Shaun was virally suppressed and could not transmit HIV to others through sex or any other kind of contact. While he was in custody, Shaun heard one of the police say, "Be careful, he's HIV positive," to a fellow officer.

"They saw my status and thought, 'Because he's got HIV, automatically, we should use the HIV laws and we should charge him,'" said Shaun. "If you're going to charge someone you guys should kind of dig in a little deeper, you know, make sure there is a risk. But it's like automatically they are looking at it like there is a risk. There wasn't a risk." He tried to explain the basics of HIV science to the police as they questioned him, but they would not listen. In their eyes, he was a risk.

The police continued to interview Shaun while he was in pain and without a lawyer for hours, asking him detail after detail about his ex-partner. Eventually Shaun was connected to a lawyer through legal aid. Many legal aid lawyers are highly qualified and knowledgeable, but unfortunately, the one assigned to Shaun was not. "He didn't know anything about the case, like he didn't know anything about HIV." The lawyer did not contest Shaun's charges or the way he was violently treated while in custody.

After voluntarily turning himself in, being assaulted, and being interrogated without a lawyer, Shaun was sent to a jail cell. He was being remanded until his bail hearing. Remand means someone is detained prior to a hearing or trial. People can be held in remand if they are denied bail because their case is institutionally considered very serious and/or if they may be deemed a risk for fleeing or a risk to others. Remand is a controversial practice, as it means someone is being incarcerated before due diligence of the system—before being found guilty or innocent—but it is a very common practice. As of 2022, 71 percent of people incarcerated in the provincial system in Ontario were on remand or incarcerated prior to being proven guilty. A disproportionate number of those are people of color.[10] In Canada, if someone is sentenced for less than two years, they are incarcerated in the provincial system. They are also incarcerated provincially under remand. After a sentence of two or more years, people are incarcerated federally.

While Shaun was jailed awaiting a hearing, the police put out a press release with a headline warning: *Police believe there may be more victims. Photograph released of man charged with aggravated sexual assault.* The media release was posted on the local police Twitter and Facebook accounts and the police website, and it was sent to multiple media outlets. It included Shaun's biometric details—his height, weight, eye and hair color, any visible identifying marks—a mugshot, and a statement asking for anyone who had sex with him to come forward. Several media articles were published after the release, which were widely dispersed online and included Shaun's name, photo, HIV-status, and the police profile of him, along with the details of his charges. The police framing of Shaun as a risk went unquestioned by the media. Shaun was not asked for a comment by any journalist, nor was his partner.

Shaun waited in jail for a month for his bail hearing. He told me he was concerned about his immigration status and that he might be sent back to Saint Vincent because of the charges. His aunt testified at the hearing, which Shaun told me was held in a small dingy courtroom with fluorescent lighting. She told the judge that Shaun was not a flight risk and had family connections in the city where he lived. She asked the judge to grant Shaun bail, appealing that he had no previous criminal record and was a good student. The judge was not persuaded and told the court, "Shaun is a menace to society."

Back in his living room, Shaun told me, "They said I was a high risk to the public, and 'If we let him out, he's just going to keep doing this again and again.'" He told me, "They treat you like your HIV is a weapon that you used to hurt someone. You're walking around with a loaded gun. They see us people with HIV as violent." Shaun was denied bail and sent to a provincial jail to await his trial.

DICHOTOMIZATION

The process of making a case begins when someone is identified to, or made to contact, authorities such as police or public health institutions. As soon as Shaun's ex-girlfriend contacted police, an institutional sequence of action was initiated to classify him as a risk that required intervention and containment. Shaun's experience, as well as that of his ex-girlfriend, was forced into a one-dimensional box that had already been determined. Institutions' initial engagements with Shaun did not seek to help him understand his circumstances or provide him with support. Rather, Shaun was violently assaulted with immunity by police, and the way they categorized him as a risky perpetrator took away his ability to access any other form of subjectivity. He was a risk, and that was that. Under this system, people who are institutionally understood as perpetrators of harm can be stripped of access to their own physical or emotional safety or security.

The experiences of Shaun and his ex-girlfriend were classified into the dichotomous logic of victim/perpetrator. This process of dichotomizing nuance serves to activate a range of legal tools and extralegal processes comprising the formal institutional aspects of criminalizing a person. As a result of Shaun turning himself in to the police, and the initial institutional interactions that followed, his story was retold in the form of a dichotomous narrative by police and the media, leading to his experience to be transformed into a criminal legal issue. The process of creating a dichotomous narrative is required by institutions for them to take criminal legal action and construct people into objects of risk.

This process of dichotomization is a product of a colonizing logic of us versus them, which also individualizes social problems. As I mentioned, in examining colonization, Frantz Fanon outlined how the colonized world is compartmentalized, and dichotomous ways of thinking and being are ontologically and epistemologically produced, such as the civilized/barbarian, the respectable/degenerate, the human/subhuman, to humanize/racialize, and the victim/perpetrator.[11] Colonization creates dividing lines where people are separated into two different species: one representing the ruling class and the other representing the underclass. Understanding one species as human and dominant and one as subhuman and subservient allows for the enactment of legitimated state violence against the underclass. The classification process that constructs the categories of human and subhuman removes any moral or ethical dilemmas or problems for the colonizer. This classification is completed through legal processes, which constitute certain groups as legal persons, guarantee the rights of personhood, and position others in precarity beyond legally safeguarded personhood. Violence can be enacted against those deemed subhuman, since they remain unprotected by the law. The colonized peoples become the object of violence rendered less than human so that those rendered legal persons can take hold of power in colonial nation-states.

This same dichotomizing logic extends to those deemed criminal. While there is no doubt that certain people cause harm, the label of criminal and criminality is an othering logic that creates dividing lines. There are criminals and the rest of us. Instead of helping to undo forms of social harm, this *us versus them* understanding of harm further extends and enables its manifestations.

None of the actions that Shaun took to protect his partner were considered or acknowledged by authorities, as they did not need to be. The process of turning Shaun's experiences into a case intentionally flattened complexity. Shaun's experiences were rendered to serve the dichotomous criminal legal system narratives of innocent/guilty and victim/perpetrator, as well as the public health logic of risk management and the policing logic of protecting public safety. The process of dichotomization is a key component of making a case and institutionally classifying people so that they can be managed, contained, and incapacitated.

The institutional sequence of action required to criminalize someone—to label them as a risk, to frame them as a violent perpetrator, to enact sanctions against them—requires that people's complex experiences be reconstituted into a narrative required by institutions. As with Shaun's experience, becoming a case relied on the creation of documents. The release from police is reproduced in the media, allegations of wrongdoing become codified, and people like Shaun are constructed as the most egregious of threats to society.

Because of the institutional conceptual construction within the criminal legal system that people with HIV pose a heightened risk, Shaun's experience of being virally undetectable, and therefore nontransmissible, on top of having used condoms, was erased. Shaun's partner immediately became viewed and understood institutionally as a victim, and he became a threat to the public. The making of a case is not a process that considers or cares for the needs or realities of criminalized people or others involved in the experience. This is not a process that seeks to produce understanding, healing, or justice for the criminalized. To make cases, people's firsthand accounts are reconstituted through the logic of institutions, with the aim of categorizing people into institutional risk categories.

LENORE

It was now deep summer in 2016. Golden-hour sun blanketed the top of a row of box stores that lit up across the sky. I spotted the yellow and red Tim Hortons sign and pulled off the freeway into the parking lot. I could have been anywhere in rural Canada, passing the same stores and generic landscaping, but the sky gave the prairies away. It seemed to go on forever. I remembered the old joke about the prairies, that the land is so flat, you could watch a dog run away for three days. Everything was so clear and grand.

I pulled up to the Tim Hortons near what initially looked like two teenagers sitting on the curb. Lenore was sitting with her boyfriend, hunched over. I got out of the car and walked over to them. A social worker had connected me and Lenore a month earlier, and I had met her earlier that day at a group drop-in health center that held a monthly group for Indigenous women living with HIV.

Lenore had said she wanted to share her experience with me, but given previous betrayals of her trust and privacy, she was reluctant to do so unless her boyfriend could join us. She needed to build trust with me, and her boyfriend's presence offered her a sense of safety and moral support. Lenore introduced us, remarking that her boyfriend was both HIV negative and white—which meant to her that he had little insight into her direct experience—but regardless, he had been a major support for her. They had met shortly after Lenore had first been criminally charged with aggravated sexual assault and he had supported her throughout her entire experience with the criminal legal system. I said hello and suggested we go into Tim Hortons to get something to eat.

After we ordered sandwiches and obligatory coffees, we found a table in the corner where we had some privacy. We made small talk at first. They told me about how they liked the same music and played in a band together in their garage. Lenore told me they were both from working-class backgrounds and grew up with limited means. It was obvious that they were in love—they were openly affectionate toward one another, and he seemed to show unequivocal support for her. She was soft-spoken and struck me as shy at first, but with an edge—a twinkle in her eye. She had been through a lot, and she told me she was burning to get it out and let it go. She jumped into telling me about her first experience with the police in her small town. I turned on my digital recorder. One day, Lenore's social worker called to tell her a RCMP officer was trying to reach her. Canada's federal police force has jurisdiction where municipal or provincial police forces do not, often in rural areas. "My social worker said, 'They need to talk to you about something. Can you come to the police station?'" said Lenore. She was scared and confused, but this was not her first time hearing from authorities.

Before the RCMP reached out, a nurse from the local public health authority had visited Lenore at her home a few times over the course of a year. The nurse had told her that public health authorities were aware that she was HIV positive. They demanded that she disclose her status to her sexual partners, but they provided Lenore with no guidance on how she should go about it.

Lenore had been in a deep depression since she learned that she had HIV about two years earlier. She had been sexually assaulted, at which time HIV was transmitted to her. The sexual assault had not been taken seriously by police, and she felt too ashamed to advocate for herself. Charges were never laid against the man who assaulted her. Lenore told me she had been partying a lot to cover up her feelings about both her HIV status and the assault. "I felt disconnected from myself emotionally and physically," she told me.

Lenore had started hooking up with a new guy. She never told him her HIV-positive status—she didn't know how to—but she told me, "I didn't feel that I was keeping it secret, either". She was virally undetectable, and she knew that she could not transmit HIV, but she was still unsure about what it all really meant. Lenore and the new guy only had sex when they were both inebriated on booze and pills. At one point, she tried to give him a condom, "but he didn't use it," she said. This was her way of disclosing. But she did not feel she had the power to assert that the condom must be used. "I was scared that if I asserted myself, he would know why I wanted him to use it," she told us sitting at the table while holding her coffee cup. It was not sex with a trusted partner, where open communication was possible—it was sex as a way of getting lost.

Somehow, the new guy was known to public health authorities, and a while later, he told authorities about his interactions with Lenore. Following that revelation, public health authorities reached out to her. HIV is a reportable communicable disease across Canada, meaning that in most cases, by law, public health authorities have access to information about who is living with the virus in their jurisdictions. Often, investigations into new cases of HIV take place to determine the level of risk for further transmissions, and if intervention is needed. That's when the nurse came knocking.

Lenore found the encounters with the public health nurse jarring and disturbing. "They didn't give me any helpful information when it came to figuring out living with HIV," she said, or on navigating power and safety dynamics with her sexual partner. And, as the nurse was white, Lenore felt she acted in racist ways, judging her as "just another drunk Indian" who needed to be controlled. Lenore told me that she believes the public health authorities were the ones who reported her to the police.

After the call from her social worker, Lenore was scared. She already felt ashamed about her sexual assault and about having HIV. But, she said, "I knew I had done nothing wrong." She went to the RCMP station with the support of her social worker. They immediately read Lenore her rights before taking her upstairs to the interrogation room. She quickly received duty counsel, a publicly available defense lawyer who she called and who told her not to say anything to the police.

The police told her she was being charged with aggravated sexual assault. She tried to follow the advice of her appointed lawyer and kept quiet. One of the detectives came in and asked if Lenore would consent to having her medical files released to police. "I was like, 'Not really.' Well, the constable said, 'If you don't consent, we are just going to do it anyways.'" The detective was right: Lenore's health care providers immediately relented to a seizure warrant and the police accessed her medical files. Her medical records now became part of her criminal case.

About an hour later, another constable that Lenore knew through her family came into the room. It was a small town, and people knew each other. "I knew his son's nephew. We had that direct relationship, so then I talked even without her lawyer present. I told him everything," she said. She told him about how she got HIV, how she had tried to turn her life around, and the abuse she'd experienced in her life. "To him, I'm like one of his other children, so he had to leave the interrogation room to go cry."

The RCMP constable that knew Lenore told her they would release her on her own recognizance. When someone is released on their own recognizance of bail, they promise to pay the court money if they fail to follow the conditions of their release. This can take place if the judge deems someone to be less of an immediate risk to the public. They released her with a promise to appear in court, telling her that nothing would happen for now, but that she remained under investigation. The next day, Lenore heard from her social worker again. Her name and picture had been printed in the local newspaper. The RCMP had released a public safety warning about Lenore to the media, asking for other "victims" of Lenore's to come forward. Lenore told me that she thought the RCMP detectives used her contact with the constable against her, getting her to disclose information that she was told not to share by her appointed lawyer. She felt angry and used. "What the fuck?" Lenore said as she recounted the story, recalling how betrayed she felt. She had trusted the constable.

Despite what the constable had told her and what she had shared about her experience, her HIV status, combined with the charge, meant the police viewed Lenore as a threat to the public. After the release of the public safety warning and subsequent sensational media reports, Lenore told the police that she was changing her address. Isolating herself felt like her only way out.

LEGAL FACTS

When someone is criminalized, the official story that is told about them is constructed from legal facts that are organized via the logic of authoritative institutions. These

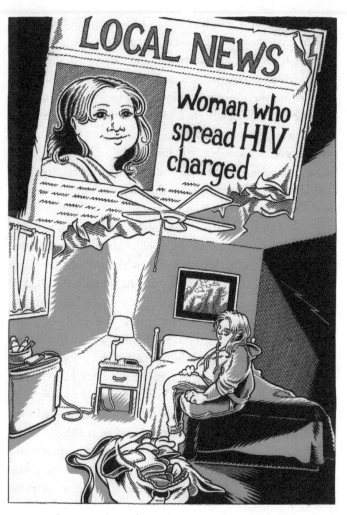

FIG. 2.3. Lenore in the media

legal facts are not necessarily grounded in what happened. As Shaun and Lenore's experiences demonstrate, the process of criminalization is not focused on actual instances of harm but on an idea of harm that can be legally regulated. Shaun was assaulted by the police. Lenore had been sexually assaulted before she was criminally charged. Neither of those harms were taken seriously by official institutions. Racist police violence and sexual violence against women are rarely a concern for criminalizing institutions. Rather, such institutions seek to manage ideological fears which are rooted in the racist and colonial legacy of othering.

The process of making a case through legal facts is necessary for criminalized people to be classified, managed, and incapacitated. Complex subjects become understood solely as objects of risk. The process strips people's experiences of their complexity and renders them to fit the abstracted logic of criminalizing institutions. Details about people's lives are organized by institutions in a way to establish, categorize, and manage certain kinds of risk. What does not fit within the institutional narrative required to criminalize someone is discarded or reconfigured. In such a context, legal facts should not be confused with what is true or untrue. Rather, legal facts are what public health institutions, police, and the criminal legal system mobilize to produce and determine legal outcomes.

Feminist legal scholar Lori Beaman-Hall examined how the practices of lawyers obscured the experiences and lives of women complainants while constructing their experiences into legal cases. Beaman-Hall explained that the "legal method" is the approach taken by lawyers to construct a legal narrative that is intelligible to other actors in legal systems. Through this approach, legal actors construct a comprehensible narrative that fits within the institutional course of action.[12] The outcome of the method, however, obscures any nuance, complexity, and actual experiences of women who engaged the legal system to support them. Beaman-Hall wanted a new way to study how women's experiences and voices were marginalized within the legal system. She noted that previous means of legal analysis had often previously relied only on written court outcome documents, "yet, the majority of the discursive practices that work to obscure the everyday experiences of women are located in lawyers' offices."[13] There had been a limited focus on the local mundane practices that acted to erase experiences of women. The concern was that how a legal narrative is constructed had been ignored by researchers, and legal outcome documents had come to be understood and reified as truth. Beaman-Hall notes, "In most cases, the client trusts that the lawyer knows what she is doing, or feels unable to challenge the legal process and, therefore, rarely asserts her right to tell her story her way."[14]

Beaman-Hall argued that the outcome of the legal method process is that women's experiences become invisible, erased, and marginalized. She further explained how the legal method works. For example, a woman named Joan comes into her lawyer's office. She tells the following story of her family: "Last night John came home and said he was leaving to live with a friend . . . I don't know why he left . . . I thought things were going alright . . . so anyway, I started crying, and then the kids started crying because they knew that I was upset . . . , he said all of this in front of the kids, you know . . . , then the kids asked me if daddy was leaving because they were bad . . . well that just made it worse, and he called me a useless bitch and then he slammed the door and left."[15]

Beaman-Hall notes that to reconstruct Joan's story as a legal issue, her lawyer will extract from what Joan has said, that Joan has a legal relationship with John, and that Joan and John are living separate and apart. The complexities of Joan's pain and suffering, or her anxieties about the children, are set aside and obscured. Those details do not fit into what is required to take a legal course of action. The story is reconstituted into a series of facts that are required to tell a legal narrative that is comprehensible to other lawyers, judges, the legal system, or experts.

For both Shaun or Lenore, the legal facts that their newly abstracted cases were reduced to were (1) they were HIV positive, (2) there was an alleged act of nondisclosure, and (3) there was a conceptual possibility that transmission of HIV could have occurred, regardless of if that transmission took place. Indeed, those are the only facts that had been required as of the 2012 Supreme Court decision to argue for a case of an aggravated sexual assault in court, and for a prosecutor, nothing else matters—including the reality that in both cases, transmission was impossible. Despite Lenore presenting a condom to her partner, she did not have the power to assert its use. The 2012 decision only focuses on if a condom was used; context or intent are evacuated. Organizing a case into a series of legal facts works to reinforce the dichotomy of victim/perpetrator, seeking only what is relevant to reinforce that framing. Whatever information does not fit within the required legal course of action is discarded as irrelevant.

The experiences of Shaun and Lenore were consistent with other people I interviewed. All but two people of the sixteen people I spoke with indicated that they were virally undetectable when the incident that led to the charges took place. Most of the people understood that being undetectable meant they could not transmit HIV sexually, and many had been told by medical professionals that being undetectable meant they could not transmit HIV. The people I spoke with told me that there was a widespread lack of knowledge of the current science of HIV by police, lawyers, and courts. This put people who were criminally charged in the position of having to educate those tasked with criminalizing them about viral load and transmission. People felt that the police's stigma and ignorance were enabled by the legal context of criminalization. This resulted in the people charged being placed in a position where they had to educate those tasked with arresting and punishing them. Often outdated information, or blatant misinformation, was communicated by people. People who needed help and support, or who caused no actual harm, were framed as extreme threats via the practices of institutions working to constitute legal facts instead of creating understanding and support.

The act of constructing a case that consists of legal facts relies on a range of sources of information from various institutions. This information stems from the criminalized individuals themselves, their sexual partners, public health authorities, the police, and health care providers. For instance, health care providers allowed the seizure of Lenore's personal medical files, which the police then used against her to prove her knowledge of her HIV-positive status. Health information is reconstituted under the logic of threat and risk to determine someone's criminality. Although, to construct these cases, basic scientific knowledge on HIV transmission was discarded, ignored, or misunderstood. As we can see in both the cases of Shaun and Lenore, legal facts can be oriented around fear, threat, and a logic of risk, often rooted in discrimination, racism, fear of sexuality, and ultimately a lack of understanding, not on the science of HIV transmission.

Furthermore, institutional racism and ignorance around communicable diseases, anti-Blackness, anti-Indigeneity, and anti-HIV discrimination and sentiments in the system toward Shaun and Lenore meant their experiences were not trusted or treated with care. The reliance on legal facts works to maintain the authority of institutions and experts. When complex experiences are reduced to legal facts, the primacy of criminal legal regimes of truth is upheld, and people's expertise regarding their own lives and experiences is marginalized.

CYNTHIA

The spring of 2017 kept unfolding. Yellow sprigs of Forsythia shot out alongside slowly blossoming buds. I was walking down the street to meet Cynthia at a park near her neighborhood in the west end of a large city. Cynthia approached me wearing sunglasses and a long soft coat, her heels clicking on the pavement of the park path.

We had been connected through a community organization but had never formally met. We said hello and made small talk about the spring weather as we headed to get coffee at a café across the street. We found a secluded bench in a corner of the park. Cynthia had a gentle demeanor. She apologized for her English, which was her third language and one she was still learning. I told her that her apologies were not necessary. She took off her sunglasses, looked up at me, and smiled as she started to tell me about her life. I turned on my digital recorder.

Cynthia was in her mid-thirties and had moved to Canada from Mexico three years earlier. "I felt that living as a transsexual woman in my home country was impossible," she said; she feared she would face life-threatening violence if she stayed. In Canada, she hoped could be herself and live as she wanted. She missed her family but was regularly in touch with one of her siblings, who was supportive and caring.

Cynthia had been working as a sex worker since she arrived in Canada. She was undocumented and concerned about her precarious citizenship status, but she was working bit by bit to establish herself. She enjoyed her work and the freedom to work whenever she wanted, and she generally liked her clients. She had a big apartment to herself and worked out of her home.

Cynthia was on HIV medication and had been since she found out her HIV-positive status a year prior. "I am undetectable, I cannot transmit the virus," she said. Despite this fact, she always used condoms with her clients. She cared about her health, and she did not want to deal with other sexually transmitted infections.

She did not disclose her HIV-positive status to her clients—"it was none of their business, plus it might be bad for business," she noted. The stigma of HIV was still significant, regardless of the realities of viral suppression and transmission. If clients knew about her status, she might get harassed online, through the websites and message boards where she advertised her services. Many of her clients had limited knowledge of HIV, and she did not feel it was her job to educate them. She knew she was not putting her clients at risk. She did what made sense to protect them and herself.

As we sat together in the corner of the park, Cynthia began telling me about how she became involved with the criminal legal system. About four months earlier, one of her regulars came over one night drunker than usual. "I did not drink or do drugs, but some of the clients like to," she said. She tolerated it to a point. That evening, Cynthia became annoyed by her client's behavior and tried to call the appointment off, asking him to leave and come back another time.

Cynthia's appeals did not work. "He pulled a knife, holding it to my neck," she said. He raped her. He did not use a condom. I asked her what happened afterward, "I was terrified, I called the police," she told me. During the police investigation, the officers learned about her HIV-positive status, and when they spoke with the man who raped her, they told him that he could press charges against her. A few weeks later, she received a letter from a detective, stating that she was under investigation and that police were considering pressing criminal charges of aggravated sexual assault.

"This man knows where I live; he had been violent to me, and now they are saying criminal charges," She was scared. She told me that because she was a sex worker, the investigation of her rape and assault was not being pursued any further by the police. Instead, she was being threatened with a charge of aggravated sexual assault for not disclosing her HIV status to her rapist.

After Cynthia received the letter about the investigation, she felt constantly surveilled, scared, and worried. She thought they would deport her back to Mexico if she was charged. And now that the client who had assaulted her knew that she was HIV positive, he had started stalking and harassing her. She was terrified in her own neighborhood, isolating herself and rarely venturing outside. She deactivated her social media accounts because he also began harassing her and her friends online.

She felt as though she had no means to protect herself, and she worried she would face additional violence from her former client. She was too scared to call the police again—they were the ones who placed her in this situation in the first place. "If I had not called them, I would not have this charge hanging over my head," she told me.

CYNTHIA HAD BEEN WORKING AS A SEX WORKER SINCE MOVING TO CANADA FROM MEXICO. AS A TRANS WOMAN WITH HIV, SHE SAID SHE FELT SAFER LIVING HER LIFE HERE.

SHE TOLD ME SHE ENJOYED THE WORK, GENERALLY LIKED THE CLIENTS, AND WORKED OUT OF HER HOME.

SHE WAS ON HIV MEDICATIONS, WAS UNDETECTABLE, AND USED CONDOMS WITH HER CLIENTS.

SHE DID NOT TELL HER CLIENTS ABOUT HER HIV-POSITIVE STATUS.

IT WAS NONE OF THEIR BUSINESS, AND IF THEY KNEW ABOUT IT, IT MIGHT ALSO BE BAD FOR HER BUSINESS.

SHE BELIEVED SHE WAS PROTECTING HER CLIENTS AND HERSELF.

ONE OF CYNTHIA'S REGULARS CAME OVER ONE NIGHT MORE INTOXICATED THAN USUAL. HE PULLED A KNIFE ON HER AND RAPED HER, HOLDING THE KNIFE TO HER NECK.

HE DID NOT USE A CONDOM.

SHE WAS TERRIFIED AND CALLED THE POLICE AFTERWARDS.

DURING THE INVESTIGATION, THE POLICE LEARNED ABOUT CYNTHIA'S HIV-POSITIVE STATUS.

WHEN THE POLICE SPOKE WITH THE MAN WHO SEXUALLY ASSAULTED HER, THEY TOLD HIM HE COULD PRESS CHARGES AGAINST HER.

A FEW WEEKS LATER, CYNTHIA RECEIVED A LETTER FROM A DETECTIVE STATING THAT THE POLICE WERE CONSIDERING PRESSING CRIMINAL CHARGES OF AGGRAVATED SEXUAL ASSAULT.

THEY DID NOT TAKE HER ASSAULT SERIOUSLY BECAUSE SHE WAS A SEX WORKER.

INSTEAD, SHE WAS BEING THREATENED WITH CHARGES FOR NOT DISCLOSING HER HIV-POSITIVE STATUS TO HER RAPIST.

IF I HADN'T CALLED THEM, I WOULDN'T HAVE THIS CHARGE HANGING OVER MY HEAD.

FIG. 2.4. Cynthia's story

When listening to the experiences of criminalized people living with HIV, it becomes clear that what comes to be institutionally understood as wrongdoing by police, public health, the courts, and the media is often much more complicated than how it comes to be presented as a case. The experiences of Shaun, Lenore, and Cynthia reveal the disjuncture between how criminalized people with HIV know the world around them and how they come to be constructed into cases. Within institutional ethnography, the disjuncture between people's own experiences and the ways in which they are conceptually understood by institutions becomes the site of research.[16] Examining this disjuncture means looking at the official conceptual forms of knowledge from institutions, texts, and experts—which act to regulate people's lives—and the unofficial and marginalized knowledge lived and embodied by people. With this approach, institutional ethnography aims to counter the reproduction of ongoing forms of imperial, epistemological, administrative, and material violence that certain people face daily via institutions.

Turning the actual into the conceptional, or translating the experiences of Shaun, Lenore, and Cynthia into institutional ways of knowing—the process of making a case—represents the point at which criminalized people then lose control over their own autonomy and future direction of their lives. There are countless complex human interactions and scenarios that arise while navigating living with HIV: making informed health care decisions; experiencing stigma, discrimination, and fear; people's inability to address their own HIV status; relationship problems or misunderstandings; disputes; and moments of silence or things that get left unsaid. Such situations are not understood based on the nuanced circumstances in the context in which they arise and from the perspectives of the people involved. From the point of arrest, people who were charged or threatened with charges described a series of events that were not marked by understanding but instead marked by HIV-related stigma, panic, discrimination, and fear.

The disjuncture that is present here between how the discursive fields of biomedical science and legal knowledge intersect lies in the notion of what constitutes "harm" when HIV nondisclosure becomes understood as a crime. Due to prevailing biomedical evidence outlining that people on HIV treatments can no longer transmit the virus to others, exposure to HIV, it can be argued, does not necessarily meet the legal threshold of the risk of imminent threat of serious bodily harm. However, the prevailing Canadian legal discourse on the issue has for years understood both exposure and nondisclosure in the context of consensual sex as a harm evaluated using the same legal tests as a violent rape involving a weapon in which the life of the "victim" is endangered. The massive epistemological disjuncture existing on this issue results in a sense of ongoing uncertainty among many people living with HIV. But experience is sidelined, and legal discourse continues to carry the most weight. This system of knowledge underscores the practices of the institutional apparatus of the criminal legal system and public health legislation, both of which wield forms of coercive power capable of suspending rights and freedoms for those living with the virus.

For Shaun and Lenore, the charge of aggravated sexual assault was shocking, since they understood the sex, they had had to be consensual. They believed that they acted in a way that protected their partners from potential transmission, such as taking their medications regularly, which rendered them noninfectious, or using condoms, or both. Conflating those actions with intent to cause harm would be much more difficult if the circumstances surrounding them were presented in all their complexity. The charge of aggravated sexual assault was extremely confusing for all the people I interviewed. Most of the people were concerned about transmitting HIV to someone else and understood that they acted in a manner to protect their partners from potential transmission, such as noting that they took their medications regularly. Inclusive of Lenore, Cynthia, and Shaun, all but two of the fourteen people who I interviewed, who had been criminally charged, indicated to me that this was their first-ever criminal charge. Despite this, all the people I interviewed who were charged, except Lenore, were denied bail due to the perceived severity of the case and were then held on remand or under house arrest for long periods. The disjuncture between what people knew about their experience and how they came to be treated and understood by institutions could not be more divergent, and the results were legal violence.

Lenore handed her partner a condom prior to sex, which he did not use. She was charged with aggravated sexual assault. Shaun had disclosed his status to his partner, who later went to the police and lied that disclosure had not taken place. He was charged with aggravated sexual assault. For Cynthia, the potential charge of aggravated sexual assault was perhaps even more confounding. During our time in the park, she asked angrily, "What am I guilty of? Being raped?" In instances like Cynthia's, a serious sexual assault was disregarded to instead manage and control an ideological harm supposedly posed by HIV. It is rare that people bring sexual assaults to police. In 2019, 6 percent of incidents were reported to police, with many fearing they would not be taken seriously by the system.[17] Cynthia's experience underscores the concerns of many. Instead of being heard, understood, and supported by the system, she was turned into a perpetrator and framed as a risk. Her experience was discarded for an institutional narrative driven by fear, stigma, and misunderstanding toward sex workers, people of color, trans women, and people living with HIV.

For authorities to enact the most serious of legal tools and usher a person into institutional processes, that person must be understood to pose an urgent problem that requires intervention and management by institutions. The more extreme the case, the more an extreme reaction becomes justified, including intensified and amplified forms of legal violence. Such an extreme classification is inconsistent with the actual experiences of these criminalized people.

The process of making a case is not the inevitable or natural outcome of wrongdoing that causes harm. Indeed, when we look at the stories of Shaun, Lenore, and Cynthia, it is hard to discern any such wrongdoing in the first place. When we listen to the experiences of criminalized people, it becomes clear that HIV criminalization is not about remedying actual wrongdoing, or about listening to science but is about punishment and retribution to demonstrate that the system is doing what it intended to do.

These experiences reveal the disjuncture between what institutions know about HIV and the actual experiences of those living with the virus. Cases are made through the dichotomization of experiences into victim/perpetrator and through official ways of knowing that promote the legal facts of a case, such as police safety warnings, court files, and media reports. The making of cases is the threshold through which legal violence comes to organize and circumscribe criminalized people's lives.

~ 3 ~

Institutions and Information

The process of criminalization relies on various pieces of information and an array of institutions. When a person is marked as a criminal and a threat to public safety, a wide range of information is produced by the authoritative institutions of policing, media, health care providers, public health authorities, criminal and public health courts, jails and prisons, and nongovernmental organizations. Examining the making of cases in relation to HIV criminalization reveals how these institutions—which are often perceived to be separate and siloed from one another, such as police and public health—can instead work together to intensify surveillance and punishment.

Independently or in concert, and sometimes in contradictory ways, institutions both distribute existing information and develop new information to construct cases. This includes press releases, public safety warnings, legal case documents, media articles and interviews, personal photographs, institutional directives, expert opinions, medical files, and police communications and interviews. The aim of sharing such information with the public is to be predictive of perceived future risks and to regulate and circumscribe behavior and opportunities. This convergence of institutions and information, and the ways that information is mobilized to make a case, can also enable forms of violence, punishment, and retribution. In this context, information about a case easily leads to racist, misogynist, and homophobic public discrimination via social media and online bulletin board posts.

The cases of HIV criminalization that have emerged over the years are often sensationalized in the media, such as that of Anna's in 1991. Her case garnered much public attention after the media publicized her name. Local community groups protested the move, calling it a breach of privacy. But the media continued. During her case, Anna escaped from her transition home. The media headline that followed was: "*Hunt on for HIV woman: Vanishes from shelter as sex-assault trial nears.*"[1] Media articles often reproduce the same simple narrative of HIV-positive people as a threat that must be contained by authorities. In cases of HIV nondisclosure, people's privacy is often widely breached, with photographs plastered across media outlets via police press releases prior to conviction. The media often act as extended arm of the state in such cases, and sensationalized headlines condemn the person with HIV—who is often racialized, gay, or a sex worker—as a criminal, a vector of disease, and dangerous, reckless, and irresponsible.

Much of media sensationalism in HIV cases is highly racialized. In examining media reporting on HIV criminalization cases across Canada, sociologists Eric Mykhalovskiy, Colin Hastings, and Chris Sanders found that almost half of all media coverage since 1989 has focused on just four African and Caribbean Black immigrant men. Many of the articles repeatedly represented as Black men as dangerous, hypersexual foreigners who pose a threat to the health and safety of primary white women and, more broadly, the "imagined Canadian nation." [2]

The stigmatizing threat posed by the media has also sometimes been taken up by community-based HIV organizations. In 2015, a young Black man's mugshot, released by police, was plastered all over the media in rural Ontario due to charges related to alleged HIV nondisclosure. In response, while not explicitly naming racism as a factor, the local HIV organization contacted media outlets and asked to have a statement added underneath his mugshot. The statement said,

> At this point in time, we are only aware of the details that have been provided to the public by the Peterborough Police Service. As always in these situations, it is important to remember that these alleged crimes that have not been proven in a court of law. It is our position that the criminal law is generally an ineffective and inappropriate tool with which to address HIV exposure. HIV/AIDS is an individual and public health issue first and foremost, and should be addressed as such. All legal and policy responses to HIV/AIDS should be based on the best available evidence, the objectives of HIV prevention, care, treatment and support, and respect for human rights.
>
> Most people living with HIV practice safer sex and/or disclose their status. It is everyone's responsibility, whether

they know their HIV status or not, to ensure that HIV and other sexually transmitted infections are not transmitted. Criminalization disproportionately places the responsibility for preventing HIV transmission on people living with HIV.[3]

This was a rare instance aiming to intervene in the dominant policing and media narrative. The approach was similar in ethos to the protest in support of the case of Anna in 1991, where communities resisted the dichotomous narrative promoted by police and the media through protesting at the newspaper's headquarters. But what did becoming a subject of criminalization do to people like Anna and the young man whose mugshot was all over the news? How were their lives changed? Answers to these questions are not often on the public record, as criminalization produces only one way of knowing criminalized people.

This chapter examines forms of epistemological violence stemming from the process of criminalization and the violent ways of knowing that result from it, including the violence of media reporting. Information is not benign but rather is used to enact legal and extralegal violence. Here, I examine forms of knowledge that help frame people as risks and threats who need to be incapacitated by authorities. I examine the notion of *interinstitutionality*—how criminalizing institutions work together to amplify a case's level of risk, an assessment that is disconnected from people's actual experiences of their lives, which turns private information into public spectacle.

Angie

In the fall of 2015, I began undertaking archival research on HIV criminalization, spending many hours in various libraries in Montreal, Quebec. As the leaves on the trees outside turned orange and red, I examined media reports from the early 2000s about a woman, whom I'll refer to with the pseudonym Angie. She had been criminally charged because of an alleged instance of HIV nondisclosure. The first headline I came across about her case read: "woman posed 'huge threat' by hiding HIV status: police."

Digging deeper into this supposed "huge threat," I read news stories that said a public health nurse had visited Angie three years prior to her arrest. The nurse was delivering a public health order that required Angie to disclose her HIV-positive status to all her future sex partners.

Angie, a white single mother in her mid-twenties, lived in a small town. According to the media, local police arrested Angie because they had received information from a concerned individual that she was not obeying the regulations imposed under the public health order that had been issued three years earlier. The lead detective in charge of the arrest said that he thought Angie "didn't care if she infected others she met while frequenting bars . . . where she was sexually active for years after testing positive." Upon Angie's arrest, the detective said that her noncompliance with the public health order justified releasing her photograph as a "public safety warning" to the media and community during a televised press conference.

After the press conference, the lead detective repeatedly presented Angie as a "huge threat" to public safety when speaking to journalists. He said she deliberately planned to have sex with people without disclosing that she had HIV. He claimed Angie was known to frequent bars and clubs to pick up men and said police had spoken to ten of her alleged partners, who all claimed they had unprotected sex with her. The detective encouraged anyone who had had sexual intercourse

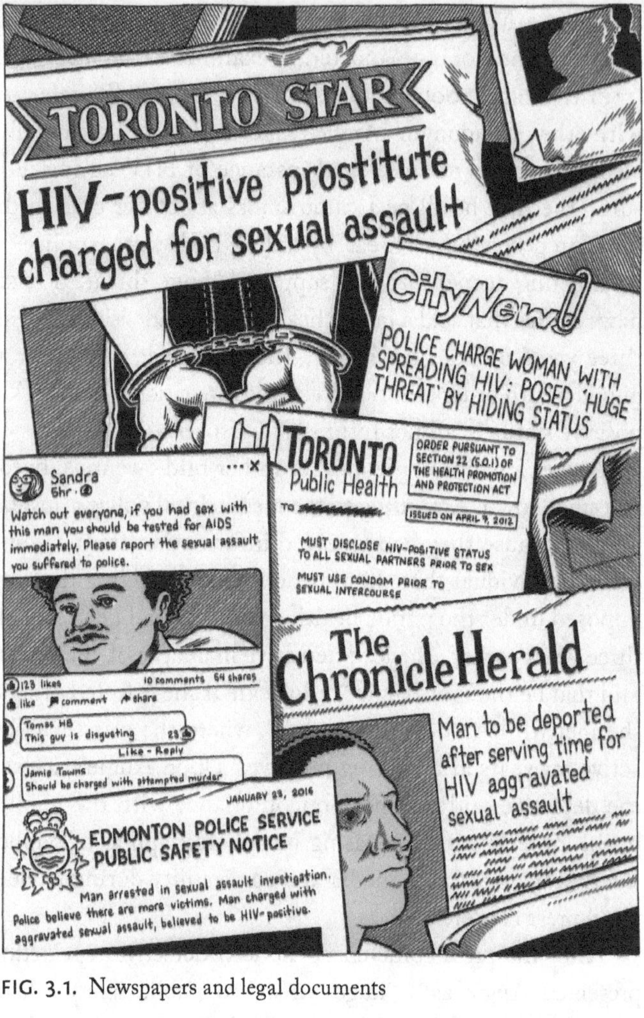
TORONTO STAR
HIV-positive prostitute charged for sexual assault
CityNews
POLICE CHARGE WOMAN WITH SPREADING HIV: POSED 'HUGE THREAT' BY HIDING STATUS
TORONTO Public Health
ORDER PURSUANT TO SECTION 22 (5.0.1) OF THE HEALTH PROMOTION AND PROTECTION ACT
TO
ISSUED ON APRIL 9, 2012
MUST DISCLOSE HIV-POSITIVE STATUS TO ALL SEXUAL PARTNERS PRIOR TO SEX
MUST USE CONDOM PRIOR TO SEXUAL INTERCOURSE
Sandra
5hr
Watch out everyone, if you had sex with this man you should be tested for AIDS immediately. Please report the sexual assault you suffered to police.
123 likes
10 comments 64 shares
like comment share
Tomas HB
This guy is disgusting 23
Like - Reply
Jamie Towns
Should be charged with attempted murder
The ChronicleHerald
Man to be deported after serving time for HIV aggravated sexual assault
JANUARY 23, 2016
EDMONTON POLICE SERVICE PUBLIC SAFETY NOTICE
Man arrested in sexual assault investigation. Police believe there are more victims. Man charged with aggravated sexual assault, believed to be HIV-positive.

FIG. 3.1. Newspapers and legal documents

with Angie to come forward and seek medical advice. When the mechanism of the public health order had seemingly failed, the police were called in to protect public health.

The name of the man who made the initial complaint about Angie was protected under a publication ban.

Meanwhile, Angie's name and face was all over the media, with the justification that the breach of her privacy was in the interest of "public safety." Online bulletin boards and discussion forums about the local nightlife scene were filled with posts sharing her photo and information, with headings such as: "Beware of HIV + female rapist," "Girl with HIV having unprotected sex with clubbers," "Lock this whore up," and "Broad has the HIV." People wrote comments that they wished to see Angie punished.

Angie's lawyer argued for her to get released with a curfew between 11:00 P.M. and 7:00 A.M. During a trip to a public pool with her young toddler, other pool goers recognized Angie's picture from a newspaper cover. As a result, she was publicly ridiculed and kicked out of the pool with her child. Angie ultimately pled guilty to one charge of aggravated sexual assault. She was sentenced to two years' house arrest and three years' probation.

One article about the outcome said Angie "cried in court today when she was told she would be registered as a sex offender for life and would be made to provide a DNA sample." The same article stated, "Prior to going into the . . . courtroom, [she] was all giggles and was ogling a picture of shirtless men in the Sun newspaper." There was a public fixation on her sex life, the idea of her promiscuity, and the notion that she had had multiple sex partners.

After more digging into media archives, I finally found the actual circumstances surrounding Angie's case—what truly led to the police to label her a "huge threat." Angie's arrest was related to only two sex acts with the same man. There was just a single complainant in the case and no other men presented evidence in court. The police's public claim that ten men were involved in the case was groundless. Angie met the sole complainant at a party in 2007 and they had intercourse using a condom. Because they used a condom, she understood that she did not have to disclose her status. They had sex again after their first encounter, and this time, the condom broke. As soon as the condom broke, Angie told the man about her HIV-positive status. He was not infected with HIV. In the end, charges of aggravated sexual assault were laid in relation to sex Angie had with one man, during which she had tried to protect them both. However, because of the way her case was presented publicly by public health authorities and the police, she became a pariah in her own community.

Media reported that Angie did not tell her sexual partner about her HIV-positive status right away because she "got scared." If this is true, her fear is not surprising.

Around the same time that she was in court, another nondisclosure case made the news. In 2007, a man from Winnipeg in the Canada prairies named Stuart Mark, age thirty-six, disclosed his HIV-positive status to his causal partner Michael Pearce. Pearce became enraged after the disclosure, hitting Mark in the head with a golf club over fifty-eight times and stabbing him repeatedly in the stomach, lungs, and liver with a knife. Pearce was sentenced to seven years for manslaughter. The media ran a story with the headline, "Man murdered over HIV status, court told."[4] In 2014, the Manitoba Superior Court granted Pearce a new trial after his defense argued that he was treated unfairly by police and had been on Tylenol 3s at the time of the murder.[5] In the context of criminalization, where an HIV-positive person can be murdered for sharing their status, it is unsurprising that people like Angie might fear disclosing their status.

Angie's sentence was not the result of her actions but instead the actions of institutions and the information that was circulated—information that was not grounded in the reality of her experience, but rather in the conceptual risk logic of institutions of policing, public health authorities, and the criminal legal system.

In her sentencing hearing, the judge mobilized trial testimony of Angie's sex partner's fear and anxiety of being potentially exposed to HIV. In one of the rare instances Angie was able to speak for herself about her experience, she was quoted in the media stating, "Nobody understands what my life is like," while crying in the courtroom.

The material impacts of criminalization that result in this context are due to the circulation of information that come from an array of institutions. The outcome can be physical and psychological violence, as well as shunning, social exclusion, loss of autonomy, and the means to realize safety and security. Angie was treated as a heightened risk to public safety due to an initial public health order. The severity of her case was exaggerated by police making an unfounded claim that there were ten complaints and identifying her to the media and community as a "huge threat" to public safety. She was harassed online due to the dispersal of the police information on her case, called derogatory names. Angie's community shunned her in the name of their supposed self-protection, at the expense of her safety and freedom. Not only was Angie put under a curfew, but she also experienced limits on her access to public space because of the impact of media coverage.

Interinstitutionality

As seen through Angie's experience, the process of criminalization implicates many more institutions than the criminal legal system. Multiple institutions construct and manage a case in relation to HIV, including criminal law, public health, policing, health care providers, and the media. Each of these institutions performs various practices and processes that establish the legal facts mobilized to construct a case and intensify the experience of criminalization.

Dorothy Smith' feminist sociology represents a paradigm shift in how we understand and examine the social world—and how relations between people are "coordinated" by an interplay of external institutions.[6] Using the broad concept of the institution, institutional ethnography offers a method for analyzing how people's daily lives and interactions are organized, mediated, regulated, and constrained through institutions.

Smith wanted to understand how actions and decisions made by institutions, and the documents institutions develop to translate the world into cases to be managed, end up organizing people's daily lives. In her analysis, social relations between people are shaped by what she called ruling relations. Ruling relations are the work of institutions. For example, despite what Angie did, the ruling relations of policing and public health, guided by institutional policies, legal precedent, and public health and criminal legislation, had ascribed her case as being a risk to the public. These institutions imposed a series of rules and regulations incapacitating Angie, limiting her ability to access freedom. The actions of these institutions which Smith would call ruling relations, driven by a logic at a deep disjuncture from Angie's own experience, dramatically impacted her daily life.

The term "institution" within institutional ethnography refers to a given complex of ruling relations under examination. Smith proposed to study ruling relations, to understand how they operate to organize what is rendered possible or impossible for people. Using this understanding, the researcher will "explore particular corners or strands within a specific institutional complex, in ways that make visible their points of connection with other sites and courses of action."[7]

Adhering to this approach, I examine the interplay of heterogeneous institutional formations; the ruling relations, comprising the criminal legal system tasked with the administration of criminalization and punishment, such as courts, policing, and enforcement; public health authorities, health care, and the medical system; the media; and community-based organizations.

Each of these different institutions is implicated in the construction of the case on Angie's experience. The legal public health order was later taken up by police to intensify the risk logic used to construct Angie as a case, which was then widely distributed in the media. The information used in Angie's case came from various intersecting institutions and mechanisms, including a public health order, criminal charges, a police press conference, a public safety warning, a curfew mandate, and media articles, which were shared widely online to a range of websites, as well as via word of mouth in her community. The proliferation of this information resulted in her being barred from a public pool, sentenced to house arrest, and labeled a sex offender for life. The forms of information produced to assist in her criminalization incapacitated Angie's ability to access freedom, privacy, and autonomy. Multiple institutions amplified the risk of Angie's case through their interinstitutional arrangements and sequences of action.

Mobilizing institutional ethnography, Colin Hastings has examined how digital media stories on many HIV criminalization cases often replicate verbatim the text of police public safety warnings. Hastings notes that "reporters' reliance on police press releases accelerates the flow of police information and reasoning into the mainstream press and cements discursive connections between HIV serostatus, criminality, risk, and moral culpability."[8] This analysis helps us understand how Information from policing is reproduced and amplified to promote ideological understandings of the experiences that lead to HIV criminalization.

Through an interinstitutional analysis, we can also examine how clinical health information is translated by police, the media, and courts to constitute someone as a risk. This approach can enable examining how medical expertise, or public health guidance, and surveillance technologies intersect with various laws to enable the criminal legal regulation of people living with HIV—for example, looking to how Lenore's medical records were provided to police without her consent and then used to support the case of her criminalization.

What does this mean when personal health information is translated and reconstituted into the realm of criminal law? This site of analysis extends from the *medicolegal borderland*, a thought space conceptualized to assist in the interdisciplinary sociological analysis of criminality as well as health and illness situated between criminology and medical sociology.[9] Using the interinstitutional analytic of the medicolegal borderland, can help examine the competing and contested discourses of the biomedical and the legal, which developed diverging understandings of the notion of harm in the context of HIV criminalization.

Mobilizing a medicolegal borderland analysis, Chris Sanders has examined the documentary practices of nurses in Ontario when taking case notes about HIV-positive patients under their care. In the context of HIV criminalization in Canada, Sanders examined how nurses take into consideration the criminal law, leaving out important details and information because of concern that their case notes may end up in criminal investigations, where "nursing practice is being infringed upon by external concerns" of the criminal law.[10] The outcome is a potential chill between healthcare providers and their patients.

Furthermore, Stephen Molldrem, examining the United States context, looked at how a diverse range of information is mobilized to construct out-of-care watch lists of people living with HIV. The watch lists include clinical health information, information from databases like LexisNexis, and social media profiles, along with collaboration with correctional and law enforcement agencies.[11] Molldrem notes that the development of the watch lists and reuses of HIV data are done without consent and are "a concern in jurisdictions where HIV nondisclosure is criminalized."

Through Angie's experience and the experiences of others, an array of institutional texts and sequences of actions intersect to heighten the vulnerabilities of criminalized people. An interinstitutional analysis enables a focus on how various institutions interact with one another to produce intensified ontologies of violence for criminalized people. This framing allows a challenge to the assumption that singular institutions—such as police, public health, media, and the criminal legal system—act independently from one another or that they operate using siloed forms of knowledge.

While much of this book focuses on the subjective accounts of individuals who have been criminalized, honoring people's lives and experiences, I also want to draw attention to the institutions that produce and enable legal violence, often leading to violent extralegal outcomes. Focusing on institutions from the perspective of those impacted by violence addresses the structural conditions that enable violence. Doing so enables an understanding that the violence that criminalized people face is shaped by the processes and actions of institutions, rather than being the mere result of individual actions. By mobilizing an interinstitutional analysis, we can better understand the ways in which criminalized people come to be simultaneously governed, regulated, surveilled, and incapacitated by a range of institutions. This convergence amplifies the punitive aspects of criminalization, leading to intensified forms of violence.

Matteo

When I met Matteo in 2017, he was still under curfew as part of the conditions of his release. He had been incarcerated for two and a half years. Because his conditions were strict, we were not able to meet in person, so we planned a time to talk on the phone. He had been charged with aggravated sexual assault three years prior. He was twenty-six years old. He had only known his own HIV status for six months when he was charged. "It is pretty fucked up that this is how Canada supports people who just find out they have HIV, by arresting them," he told me.

We got in touch because Matteo had seen a poster about my project that I had posted on what was formerly called Twitter, which had in turn been printed out and shared in the office of a legal clinic. One of his conditions was that he was not allowed to use social media. Initially, Matteo had texted me on the burner Nokia flip phone that I had purchased for the project. For me, a smartphone was too risky. I needed a way for people to reach me, but I wanted to limit the amount of unnecessary information I was collecting on people to help protect their anonymity and confidentiality.

FIG. 3.2. Matteo under curfew

It was afternoon and I was sitting in front of a window in my living room. Light streamed in as I set up my digital recorder. Matteo called one minute before the time we had agreed upon. His voice was low and somewhat muffled, speaking in a hushed tone. He was whispering as if he did not want to be overheard. He explained that since his release, he constantly felt he was being surveilled. He told me that we were talking on the three-year anniversary of his HIV-positive diagnosis. I congratulated him on his HIV anniversary, somewhat jokingly. It's an odd thing to celebrate, but it's still an important occasion to mark. We both laughed a little.

Despite his hushed tone, Matteo spoke with confidence. He felt he had been treated unjustly by the criminal legal system. As part of his release conditions, he was mandated by the parole board to live with his parents. He was a gay Italian man who was still in college, and the conditions of his release only allowed him to leave his parents' house to attend school during the day. "I have to be escorted by my parents to and from school, I'm not really allowed anywhere else," he said. His parents were supportive, and he loved them, but he felt like he was constantly under watch by both them and the police. Being on the sex offender registry exacerbated his sense of being surveilled, "it feels like it might never go away, even though I've already served my time," he told me.

Prior to being charged, Matteo regularly used hook-up applications like Grindr and Scruff. The apps let him be social, meet guys, and occasionally hook up with them. About a few weeks prior to his arrest, he hooked up with a guy from Grindr. "I didn't tell the guy about my HIV-positive status—I wasn't sure how to go about sharing that information with someone else."

Matteo's doctor told him that since he was virally undetectable, it was impossible for him to transmit HIV. When he had first tested HIV positive, the clinic asked him to attend public health counseling. But the counseling promoted what he felt were odd and out-of-date practices, such as using condoms for oral sex, which is not necessary when someone is virally undetectable. Matteo had already learned about HIV and sexual health from a local community AIDS organization and from his doctor. That information informed his decisions when he hooked up with the guy from Grindr.

The public health counseling did not align with what Matteo had learned from HIV and AIDS organizations. He knew he was virally undetectable and not able to transmit the virus. Despite this fact, the public health nurse treated him as though he was highly contagious and dangerous. He told me, "The public health people seemed homophobic, like they had fears of gay sex," and what they promoted was out of touch with his actual needs and practices. It made him feel pathologized and bad. He had concluded, based on what he had previously learned from the community AIDS organization, that, as he told me, "I only had to disclose my status if there was a risk of transmission, and there wasn't." Matteo understood he could not transmit the virus and acted based on accurate scientific information.

Matteo had not grown-up fearing HIV. He came of age after the era of mass death and hysteria—one where the virus was rarely talked about anymore, and understandings and fears around the risk of transmission, for some gay men, had changed. Discussions between guys online about risk and sexually transmitted infection were rare. Also, Matteo was not used to talking about his status since it was still so new. He did not want to burden hook-ups with information that seemed so personal. Plus, as he understood it, by taking his medication and being undetectable, he was taking care of himself and others.

A few weeks after that Grindr hook-up, Matteo was at work in a store in the suburbs. There was a commotion up front and one of his coworkers called out his name. The police were there asking for Matteo. Before he knew it, the police had arrested him in front of his coworkers and

Many of his past friends stopped keeping in touch or shunned him once he was in jail. Through online searches, I discovered that news stories about Matteo's case had also been shared on a white supremacist bulletin board, using homophobic language and calling for violence against him. Along with promoting anti-Black and anti-Semitic hate and attacks, such websites had been used as a place to dox and vilify queer and trans people, targeting them to support ongoing hate and violence. Matteo became alienated and had no way to challenge his charge in the public sphere. The guy Matteo had hooked up with through Grindr was HIV negative and remained so—there was never any allegation that Matteo had transmitted the virus.

Eventually he decided to plead guilty to one charge of aggravated sexual assault. He was scared that if he went to trial, he would be found guilty. "I didn't trust the system, I was ashamed of all of it, and pleading guilty meant I could serve a shorter sentence" he told me. He was worried about missing his family. After his sentencing hearing, Matteo was ordered to provide a sample of his DNA and to register, for life, under the federal Sex Offender Information Registration Act.

Matteo went on to tell me about his life after being released from prison. He had a long list of release conditions: he was not allowed to use social media or any dating and hook-up apps, including Grindr, Scruff, or Tinder. He was barred from socializing in the gay community or going out to participate in social events. He was not allowed to own, use, or possess a computer or device that would allow access to the internet, unless there was written authorization by a parole supervisor (his supervisor did not allow it). He also had to report names and contact information of all his male friends to his parole officer, who would then call those friends to verify who they were. Matteo was also not to purchase or consume alcohol—a standard condition put on almost everyone who is released, even though Matteo did not even care for alcohol and rarely drank the stuff. He had to take HIV medications as prescribed by a doctor and follow a sex offender treatment plan for "sexual deviancy," which he reluctantly attended each week. "The woman who runs the group doesn't even know why I'm there," he told me. "She says I don't belong in the group, that I don't meet the criteria of a sex offender, but I have to go anyhow."

The condition that most bothered him was that he was mandated to contact his parole officer before any potential sexual conduct, providing them with the name and contact information of the person he intended to hook up with. The parole officer would then directly call the person and verify that they knew Matteo's HIV-positive status and that they consented to having sex with him. "Like, who is going to want to do that? How am I going to meet anyone?" He felt extremely isolated and lonely.

Interinstitutional Risk Logics

Through the interinstitutional interplay of criminalizing institutions, the intersection between health, sex, and crime also comes to heighten and intensify conceptions of risk. Risk is used as a technology to further criminalization processes, the outcome of which are forms of governance targeted at preempting and arresting future ideological or actual harms, such as incarcerating Matteo on remand, and communicating widely about his potential risk to public safety.

In the context of criminalization, risk is rarely equated with actual harm; rather, the idea of risk is mobilized at preemptively managing outcomes or managing an ideological harm. From this perspective, the idea of risk is mobilized to make possible the criminalizing rationality of institutions.

To activate the most serious of legal tools and to enter institutional processes, people must be understood as urgent problems who require intervention and management by state actors. The simultaneous interaction of multiple logics of risk—that is, a public health risk coupled with a criminal risk—leads to a case becoming understood as the most extreme of risks. And as I noted previously, in the context of HIV, institutional conceptions of risk can be divergent from the actual scientific realities of HIV. When someone has been marked as a risky individual by multiple authoritative institutions, the intersection of multiple risks increases the understood severity of the case.

In both Matteo and Angie's constructed cases, this risk calculus was further amped up via sensationalistic, populist, and moralizing means online and on social media. Disjuncture is apparent in Matteo's experience, where the police who arrested and charged him did not understand the biomedical risks involved. Fundamentally, the police tasked with framing Matteo as a risk were not aware of the current science behind the actual risks of HIV transmission (of which, in Matteo's case, there was no risk). Regardless of what he told the police, because he is HIV positive and gay, they understood him only as a risk, a threat, and a perpetrator. The institutional imperative to construct cases such as Matteo's as hyper-risks—via the confluence of fears around sexuality and communicable disease—supersedes the actual experiences at hand. Matteo faced a charge of attempted murder, was denied bail, and was incarcerated before even being tried and later faced harsh release conditions and surveillance, which continued to frame him as an infectious threat and did not account for his actual experience. He had the additional unhelpful and stigmatizing experience of going through public health counseling, which was also out of touch with his lived reality.

Similarly, the institutional understanding of Angie's case necessitated her being perceived as a "huge threat" despite the lack of concrete evidence to back that up. Mobilizing the notion of exception enables institutional actors to increase the risk level of a case: the greater the exception, the greater the risk and, therefore, the greater the justification for enacting forms of legal violence. In both Angie's and Matteo's cases, criminalizing institutions constructed them into violent perpetrators and risks to public safety when no violence, intent to cause violence, or actual harm occurred.

Not only was there often no intent to do harm—following the Judeo-Christian tradition of determining guilt through *mens rea* (Latin for "guilty mind")—but Angie and Matteo also actively worked to mitigate harm. From what we know, Angie had initiated condom use; when it broke, she immediately disclosed her health status. Matteo took steps to protect his partner by regularly taking medications so he would be rendered noninfectious and unable to transmit the virus. Matteo knew he could not transmit HIV and acted on up-to-date information from his local HIV and AIDS support organization.

Furthermore, policing, the criminal legal system, and public health actors can also work together to scale up people's cases to the criminal realm. In the eyes of criminalizing institutions, the subject of criminalization merely becomes an object onto which legal violence is enacted. When the criminalized speak, they are never enabled a subjectivity that allows them to be listened to or heard. Instead, they are a risk and a threat, one from which the mythical public must be protected.

Lenore

Listening to Matteo's experience reminded me of my recent conversations with Lenore, who I first met at Tim Hortons with her boyfriend. The day after we met for coffee and sandwiches, Lenore invited me over to her house. She and her boyfriend liked to play music in their garage, and we sat outside under the open door of the building. It was getting close to the end of the day and the sun had started to set, shining through the garage's small dusty windows and casting dramatic shadows. Lenore told me she thought the RCMP detectives used her family's connection with one of the constables against her. She believes the police exploited that personal connection to get her to disclose information to them, even though she had been told not to say anything by her appointed lawyer. She felt angry and used.

The day after she spoke to police, the RCMP released a public safety warning about her to the media. She told me she thought one of her high school teachers had leaked her graduation picture to the media. She had been proud of that picture before—it was an accomplishment in her family to have graduated high school. Now, the picture was tainted. The photograph was everywhere, running beside headlines in the local paper saying she had HIV and was being charged with aggravated sexual assault.

She told me, "I come from a small town, so everybody knows everything. The quiet girl is all of sudden a big media star. I felt very violated, I was told by my doctors and by the police that I'm innocent until proven guilty. It's my right to disclose. Those rights were taken away."

The constable had initially told Lenore that her case was not serious and that she would be released into the community. Yet HIV discrimination, combined with the charge of aggravated sexual assault, led her to be seen as an intensified threat to the public. The RCMP asked that people who had sex with Lenore to come forward, since she was a public health risk who had been promiscuous. "Reporters, reporters, and more reporters" immediately picked up the story, she said. They tried to contact her and her family. The media claimed she was knowingly trying to transmit HIV.

Lenore's boyfriend sat close by as she spoke and kept his hand on her leg to comfort her. She told me how the police had released her after her first interrogation. Unsure and scared about where to go and what to do, she initially went to her mother's house. She started getting threats on social media and people posted nasty and stigmatizing comments on her Facebook account. Scared, she deleted her account, even though social media was one of the only ways she kept in touch with her family members who lived in rural Indigenous reserve communities up north. Isolating herself felt like her only option—she was ashamed and wanted to disappear.

She also felt unsafe in her neighborhood and worried that her neighbors had seen the news. She decided to check into a motel in another town, waiting for her case to move forward in the courts. She borrowed her mother's car and went into a period of self-imposed social isolation out of fear.

Despite ongoing pressure from the police and her lawyer, as well as a desire to see her son and other family members, Lenore did not want to plead guilty. "I was terrified and felt

I had no support from the legal system," she told me, "my lawyer acted like a bully, he didn't know anything about HIV, he wouldn't listen to me." But she wanted to persevere and challenge the charge of aggravated sexual assault, "if anything, I was the one who was assaulted," she told me, referring to the experience that led to her acquiring HIV.

Private Information Turned Public Spectacle

Like Lenore, Matteo, and Angie, many of the people who have been constructed into HIV nondisclosure cases face sensationalist media coverage labeling them as violent predators and threats to the public. News articles often transmit false information, like that people had intentionally tried to transmit HIV to their partners. The dispersion of information from police and the media is presented as a form of public protection—that is, as a warning about risky individuals. The people who come to be constructed as cases immediately lose their rights to privacy, as intimate details about their lives spread into the public realm, including their HIV-positive status, biometrics, and criminal charges.

In the age of the internet, news articles are now available forever. The perennial and pervasive nature of the internet and indexing of news stories via search engines such as Google has multiple negative impacts on people's lives and frequently leads to social isolation due to stigma, shame, and discrimination.

Because of the media surrounding cases like Lenore's—and the anti-Indigenous racism and HIV stigma shaping public perception on her case—criminalized people like Lenore have limited access to privacy and safety in their communities. Lenore's personal photograph was leaked to the media after the police went public with her case.

Sharing this information with the public ultimately serves to crowd-source the process of criminalization, policing, and surveillance, enabling a populist engagement with cases. Publicizing a case also feeds into the necessary perception that institutions protect the public from threats. This all serves to provide evidence that criminalizing institutions are doing their jobs of protecting the public, maintaining and reproducing the logic and operations of these authoritative institutions.

Jackson

A few years before I started my archival research, there had been a development in one of the most well-known cases of HIV nondisclosure in Canada. I examined the case the same day I was researching Angie's story at the library. The man who I'll refer to with the pseudonym Jackson, a Black man was then fifty-seven years old and had been born in Uganda. He had been imprisoned and was convicted in 2009 of two counts of first-degree murder, ten counts of aggravated sexual assault, and one count of attempted aggravated sexual assault. This was the only known case in the world where someone had been convicted on charges of first-degree murder for being alleged to knowingly transmit HIV to someone else.

Jackson's case fit the racialized trope promoted widely by the media of a Black man from somewhere else putting white women at risk. Pictures of Jackson appeared under headlines like "Killer Has High Libido, Threat to Reoffend," feeding into ongoing racist and xenophobic fears of a highly sexualized immigrant outsider who preys on white women and needs to be incapacitated to protect the public. The Crown prosecutor presented eleven white women as sex partners of Jackson, all of whom claimed that he had not disclosed his HIV-positive status. Seven of these women acquired HIV, although there was no scientific evidence proving they acquired HIV from Jackson. Two of the women died of AIDS-related cancers. The two that died had not previously tested HIV positive and were not under the care of medical professionals.

Canada is a country with supposed universal access to health care, a generally robust HIV-testing infrastructure, and insurance-supported access to HIV medications. The women in Jackson's case were left behind by the health infrastructure, a common occurrence for women living with HIV. Yes, they may not have acquired HIV had they not encountered Jackson. But, also, had they been supported by the health care system, they would no doubt still be alive today. Rather than being seen as a failure of the health care system to meet the needs of women living with HIV, Jackson was individually responsible for their deaths, letting the system off the hook in the process.

Jackson was ultimately sentenced to life imprisonment with no possibility of parole for twenty-five years in 2009. In 2011, the Crown prosecutor decided to pursue marking him with the contentious label of *dangerous offender*. In Canada, being labeled as a dangerous offender means that the individual is held preventatively for an indefinite period—beyond the prison time determined by a judge for their sentence—under the justification that it is in the interest of public safety. As of 2021, there were over 1,047 people deemed to be dangerous offenders in Canada. People imprisoned as dangerous offenders are held in forms of segregation, often a version of solitary confinement. The classification of dangerous offender is highly racialized and marked by ongoing colonization, as notably,

Indigenous people account for around 5 percent of the Canadian population but represent 36 percent of those labelled as dangerous offenders.[12] Other statistics on racialization and dangerous offenders are not collected by Canadian prison authorities, although in the province of Ontario, Black adults made up about 5 percent of the adult population but accounted for 14 percent of the jail population.[13]

While Jackson was already going to be incarcerated for a long time due to his convictions, the Crown prosecutor was concerned that he may still be able to access parole in the future. The hearing to have Jackson classified as a dangerous offender was widely covered in the media. In court, it was noted that "as long as the offender's *past* conduct, whatever it may be, demonstrates a *present* likelihood of inflicting harm on others, the dangerous offender designation is justified" (my emphasis). The Crown prosecutor followed this logic and argued that Jackson's past behavior posed a future threat to public safety, citing Jackson's previous engagements with public health authorities.

In the early 2000s, Jackson allegedly had not been compliant with orders from public health that required that he disclose his status to all sex partners, use a condom for penetrative sex, and provide public health nurses with the names and contact information of all his sex partners. The Crown prosecution subpoenaed public health nurses who had counseled Jackson on the public health order to provide testimony in the hearing, along with a forensic psychiatric witness named Dr. Klassen. The psychiatrist examined Jackson before the hearing and then used Jackson's past noncompliance of the public health order to state that Jackson was a threat to the public in the future, noting that he presented "a substantial risk to the community."[14]

In his defense, Jackson's lawyers argued that the public health–mandated counseling he had received was inadequate, racist, and culturally inappropriate. It had not accounted for Jackson's cultural heritage and religion. In Uganda, where he was raised, there was no education on sex, sexual health, or sexuality. Jackson also noted that he had experienced a great deal of HIV stigma and did not know how to talk about sex or HIV. He also said he believed the verdict from his previous trial had been racist and driven by AIDS phobia. Because of how much negative media attention his trial had garnered, he felt he would never have to disclose to another person again due to his personal life being so public. Jackson told the court, "I am a man of consciousness. I listen to it. It is clear, unambiguous, and unmistakable. I had no intention to deliberately pass on my HIV to anyone." Out of desperation, Jackson told the judge he planned to get HIV tattooed on the palms of his hands so women he meets know he is HIV positive.

The judge ruled in favor of the Crown prosecution, deciding based on his history that he presented a future risk to public safety. Jackson is now a dangerous offender and is detained indefinitely as a preemptive measure. In his case, past information developed by public health authorities was mobilized in a criminal legal context to intensify his punishment and incapacitation. In Jackson's case, the institutional understanding and framing of his case stood in for his own subjectivity. When he was able to speak for himself, he was not heard or understood. The mark of criminalization and the process of dichotomization constructed him into the most heinous of violent perpetrators.

Jackson's case harkened back to an early and much-publicized case of a Black migrant from Africa—that of Charles in 1991. When he was charged, Charles, then a thirty-four-year-old Ugandan immigrant, was accused of three counts of criminal negligence causing bodily harm. According to the court, his charges were due to knowingly transmitting HIV to three white women from Ontario with "the AIDS-causing virus" between 1989 and 1991. Like Jackson's case, a media and moral panic ensued. On February 12, 1990, the medical officer of health for Middlesex-London, Ontario, Dr. Douglas Pudden, issued the city's first order under Section 22 of the Ontario Health Promotion and Protection Act toward Charles. The order forbade him from "sexual acts that involve any penile penetration into [his] mouth or anus, or into the mouth, anus or vagina of another person."[15]

During the trial, Charles's legal team argued that he had not disclosed his condition to his sex partners because he suffered from a mental illness and posttraumatic stress caused by the horrors of civil war he had faced in Uganda. His defense argued that Charles was too mentally ill to appreciate the consequences of his behavior and so was not criminally negligent due to his past trauma. In the courtroom, Charles told the judge that he was "not in his right mind."[16]

Charles's sexual relationships with white women stirred up racist tropes of hypersexualized Black men, the diseased immigrant outsider, and the noncompliant HIV-positive predator. Anti-Black and xenophobic racism underwriting the case led scholar James Miller to reformulate the acronym for AIDS as "African Immigrant Damnation Syndrome."[17] The case was highly sensationalized and controversial among HIV activists. In communities of people living with HIV, the panic resulting from Charles's case circulated around the extent to which public health and criminal laws could be mobilized to restrict people's rights. Who else would these laws target? What were people's moral, legal, and ethical responsibilities? What role did community-based organizations have in informing their constituents of these legal developments? Notable journalist, feminist, and social activist June Callwood, who has been called "Canada's Conscience" and a "national icon" and was a cofounder of Toronto's first AIDS hospice, Casey House, authored a book condemning Charles's action, entitled *Trial without End: A Shocking Story of Women and AIDS*.

In the book, Callwood referred to one of Charles's sex partners as having "the face of an angel"[18] while referring to Charles himself as a criminal, diseased, immigrant, Black, and not from here. Callwood was very vocal during the trial, calling the public health ban prohibiting Charles from having sex "a joke."[19]

Charles's case marked a moment when populist racist panic about AIDS dominated, and even members of the HIV movement worked in concert with authoritative institutions to produce knowledge that advanced the regulation, control, and criminalization of people living with HIV. Glen Brown, a spokesperson for AIDS ACTION NOW!, also agreed that the existing legislation was inadequate and may not prevent persons "from reckless, AIDS-infected people."[20] Mike Sauer, spokesperson for the AIDS Committee of London, who was supportive of Charles being criminalized, stated, "If there's not a decision, there will be all kinds of people who get nothing."[21]

Charles died before the outcome of his trial could be determined, with the *Toronto Star* running an article with the headline "Can't Convict a Ghost."[22] Callwood's book was titled *Trial without End* because, due to his death, the decision of the judge was never publicly presented.

After his death, several past sex partners of Charles's sued the state for compensation and won, noting that public health officials had been negligent in protecting the public from contagion.

Charles's case was comprised of public health orders, court documents, criminal charges, media articles, true crime nonfiction, and the comments and perspectives of HIV activists. The case demonstrates how public health, policing, criminal legal systems, and the media become intertwined and work in interinstitutional ways. Medical and public health information can be mobilized to heighten a risk management logic, one that requires coercive and punitive means. A case can come to be no longer solely a public health risk but also a criminal risk, where the target of criminalization receives sanctions from both governing institutions. Criminal laws and public health laws intersect and reinforce one another.

To further increase a case's level of risk, which leads to amplified forms of punishment, the private information of criminalized people is transformed into a public spectacle. Here we see the violence of media reporting, one that perpetrates and amplifies the violence of racism, and the epistemological violence through erasure and unknowing. Media representations of a particular case can also lead to direct personal forms of violence in the lives of those criminalized. Information about a person and their case proliferates, details about people become public, and those individuals become recognizable in their own communities. Social media and online posts disclose information and charges, encouraging if not asking the community to "watch out" for those criminalized. Moreover, information can be dispersed and mobilized to discriminate against or enhance surveillance.

In this context, public health legislation cannot be easily understood as a form of jurisprudence applied in a silo. Interinstitutionality helps to explain how interconnected the differing institutions and their rules are, illustrating that HIV criminalization is not simply a discreet criminal law issue or an issue solved via public health laws. Explicating the complexity of systems of legal violence helps frame responses while challenging the assumption that public health institutions, policing, community-based organizations, and criminal law institutions act distinctly from one another. HIV criminalization is much more complex and intertwined. That is, it is not simply a matter of criminal law.

Finally, it is important to reflect on how criminalized people only come to be known because of the processes of criminalization. I would not be writing this book had these people not been criminalized. This book is implicated in the production of information on criminalized people, and is based on how information, developed by institutions, is shared, activated, and mobilized. Perhaps my intentions to counter criminalization matter, but perhaps they do not. None of these people would be known, remembered, documented, categorized, or collected had they not been criminalized. Will more information aid in the project of undoing legal violence? Can nuance and subjectivity help render lives more complex than the simple dichotomous boxes produced through criminalization? Can we undo the world that only knows and understands HIV-positive people as others and a class of people to be protected from? Can we make our lives unrecognizable and unknowable to the simplicity of criminalization?

∼ 4 ∼

A Typology of Violence

All people marked as criminal in Canada are vulnerable to violence. However, the intersection of HIV and criminal sexual assault charges provides unique insight into the materiality of living in a negative relation to the law. A result of becoming a case through intersecting forms of institutional information enables criminalization to be a process of violence. Here, violence begets myriad forms of violence, upon more and more violence. While criminalization can be a universalizing experience for people, the ongoing social stratification of inequity, including colonization and systemic anti-Indigenous and anti-Black racism, means that the material outcomes of criminalization are not universal.

This chapter focuses on the violent material outcomes of criminalization and how they extend out beyond formal institutional punishments into a broad range of populist forms of violent retribution, social marginalization, and discrimination. Following the work of Gultang, I outline a typology of violence, the purpose of which is to disaggregate the complex forms of violence enacted against people labeled and constructed as criminal and public health risk cases. I look at the forms of violence from the state, violence from individuals, direct, structural, legal, and extralegal forms of violence that emerge as a case moves through the various processes of the criminal legal system. I use typology to examine the process of deconstituting legal personhood. Many legal protections entitled to persons (e.g., subjectivity, privacy, autonomy, freedom of movement) are no longer available to criminalized people, as they come to live a life of negative personhood. Without the protections pertaining to a person, people can become objects on which violence can be enacted with impunity. And justified forms of state violence that comprise sanctioned punishments result in an array of unsanctioned forms of violence that exist in a liminal gray area.

My task in the sections that follow lies in explaining the relationships between types of violence, to make sense of them and to put into question the process of enacting legal violence as a solution to address social problems. Multiple violence typologies have been developed for varied purposes. Some scholars have developed typologies of violence to explore and understand forms of interpersonal violence and domestic violence.[1] Psychologists working in the criminal legal system developed and now mobilize typologies of violence to institutionally categorize people as certain types of risks.[2] A common thread running through each of these typologies of violence is the desire to categorize people according to the forms of violence they enact on others. This mobilizes violence committed in the past as a diagnostic tool and as a predictor for future forms of violence. In some cases, such typologies classify people institutionally and determine the institutional course of action. For example, if someone is understood as a violent risk to the public based on past actions, they could be labeled as a risk of committing future crimes—such as with Jackson being labeled a dangerous offender. In these instances, violence becomes individualized and removed from the social context in which it develops, is facilitated, and takes place. I do not seek to take on this sort of analysis or typology of violence.

There have also been typologies of violence designed to explore and understand forms of violence in society, such as Galtung's work, which aims to make distinct structural violence from interpersonal forms of violence. Galtung had a broad definition of violence and explored a series of distinctions, modes of influence, or dichotomies that characterize violence beyond structural violence, including physical and psychological violence, direct or indirect violence, and personal and structural violence. Examining these types of violence remained important to Galtung, such that he could examine their relationships to one another. This also allowed him to understand how forms of violence can presuppose or constitute one another.

Prior to his work, there had been a limited understanding of violence as more than just direct physical or psychological violence. Structural violence is not a case of simply understanding physical or direct violence. Structural violence may be the outcome of a process or lack of action, or it could be unintended or latent, and the origins of structural violence may be obscured or obfuscated through the actions of systems and institutions. Thus, through his work on disaggregating forms of violence and making distinctions about different types of violence, Gultang questioned the relationship between structural violence and individual violence, asking, "Is there really a distinction between personal and structural violence at all? . . . Does not one presuppose the other?"[3]

Examining the forms of violence experienced in the individual daily lives of criminalized people can analytically pinpoint the origins of violence, the material impact of that violence, and how individuals resist and challenge. I explore legal punishments, including the process of incarceration, and resulting extralegal punishments, such as being denied housing and employment, as well as facing a wide range of physically and emotionally violent consequences such as beatings and verbal abuse. This analysis allows an understanding of how some forms of violence may come to be considered justifiable, while other forms of violence are not and can help to hold up to contestation the consequences of legal and justified forms of violence.

This typology of violence focuses on violence enacted toward criminalized people, but with one caveat: while the focus here is situated on individual accounts of violence using the firsthand experiences of criminalized people, I aim not to individualize forms of violence but rather to link the violence experienced by individuals to a broader system organized by institutions. Although my analysis aims to disaggregate forms of violence, I reveal that those forms are deeply intertwined, reliant upon and constitutive of each other, and intimately connected.

Finally, this chapter bears witness to violence, not to classify or categorize with a fetishistic academic gaze of calculation and extraction, but rather with the intention to hold violence to account, to render forms of avoidable suffering and the violence of criminalization unnatural, unacceptable, and open to change.

Shaun

After coffee at his place, Shaun and I went out to walk his dog around the courtyards of his suburban high-rise concrete complex. It was early in the day, and the spring sun was streaming across the suburban concert sprawl. We walked down a path next to his building, chain-link fence on either side of us. Shaun's dog was rambunctious but well behaved, diligently following Shaun's direction. Shaun looked over at me, the sun in his eyes, and continued telling me about what happened. Shaun had been denied bail. He was immediately incarcerated in a provincial jail before his trial with a random collection of men facing all types of charges. This was a recurring thing I heard during interviews. Many of those charged due to allegations of HIV nondisclosure had no prior criminal history, yet were denied bail and immediately incarcerated, and for long periods of time before their trials, if a trial occurred at all.

Like Shaun, many of the people with whom I spoke came from working-class backgrounds with limited means to access the high costs of seeking justice. The cost of a lawyer was high, and for Shaun, he had to make do with free counsel provided by the system via legal aid. For other people I spoke with, they had good experiences with their legal aid lawyers, saying they were well informed about the science of HIV and worked hard to support people, but often the issue was time. Legal aid lawyers had a high caseload and were underpaid. But Shaun's experience was different. While his lawyer also had little time for him, Shaun felt the lawyer accepted the idea that he was a dangerous perpetrator. Also, the lawyer also did not know anything about the science of the virus. Shaun told me, "The lawyer was like a dump truck. He didn't know anything about the case, like he didn't know anything about HIV. He never even brought up anything about my viral load that was undetectable up in my case for my defense and that was the one reason why I was prosecuted."

Shaun lost his trial. He was sentenced to four and a half years. He was quickly moved to a different prison and put in the general population. During his first few months, he had a hard time accessing his HIV medications, telling me, "They didn't have my pills, they just didn't have my pills." He was confused because he had been following his doctor's orders and remaining virally undetectable. Prior to being incarcerated, Shaun had been taking his medication every day. Yet, the police and court treated him like he was a threat. The institutions that framed him as an infectious risk were now denying him the very treatment that he needed to remain healthy and to suppress the virus in his body. There was no reason provided as to the delay. He was not sure if it was due to poor logistics or management of the supply, or if the prison staff were purposely trying to destabilize him. In Canada, there is an institutional directive for federal prisons that mandates that incarcerated people are to be guaranteed the same access to health care services as anyone else. This was not the case with Shaun. After two months, he finally got his pills. He was sure that during that time, his viral load had shot back up. He was relieved to get them, so he could keep managing his condition.

We kept walking, and I put the digital recorder in my shirt pocket. Inside prison, as well as not getting access to his medicine, he started facing harassment. Prisoners made comments about him being a rapist and were asking why he took medication. He realized this was because staff at the institution had been regularly breaching his privacy. Under another federal institutional directive from the Canadian government, prisoners' charges and health status should remain confidential, and the only people who could get access to the information are guards. He told me, "One time a sheriff was transporting me from jail to court and there were a bunch of other guys, and then he said, 'Put the guy with the sexual assault over there.' Like, everyone heard, and it was already in the newspaper. Then the staff started leaving my transport papers around . . . they are supposed to put them in the locked desk, but anyone could walk by and read it, so I started freaking out."

The papers identified his criminal charges, information about his health status and his medications. Ultimately, after days of harassment, he was attacked by other prisoners while trying to call his lawyer. They surrounded him, pushed him to the ground, and started kicking. "They said they knew I was trying to spread the virus," Shaun said, while the guards watched and did nothing to intervene for a long period of time. He was certain that the guards had leaked information about his charge to the prisoners, knowing he would be assaulted. There was no other way for the information to end up in the hands of other prisoners. He told me angrily, "I was getting beaten by all the inmates. 'Cause the correctional officers and the bailiffs had disclosed my charge to people on the range, I got beat up, and they put me into, I can't remember what they called it, protective custody."

The range is the cellblock that is shared by a group of prisoners. Shaun was moved to administrative segregation, which meant he was isolated from human interaction. Segregation meant most of the day alone in his cell, with thirty minutes, or sometimes a little more, outside. While he would no longer be attacked, he spent hours alone, getting depressed and feeling hopeless. He was not allowed any clothes and only had a concrete floor with no bed until nighttime. He was given just one sheet of paper and a pencil to occupy his time while locked down alone in a cell.

Shaun continued his story. We sat on a bench under a tree. He told me how hard it was to see a doctor while in prison. At seemingly random intervals, and much less frequently than when he was not incarcerated, Shaun was taken to see his doctor, an HIV specialist at a hospital an hour's drive from the prison. This time, after months of asking for his routine blood tests, he thought his appointment was finally going to be granted. He wanted to make sure being denied medications from the prison officials had not impacted his health. He was transported to the hospital, accompanied by guards, this time to a place different from where he normally received care. Shaun was brought into the hospital wearing his orange jumpsuit, a suit that made him feel ashamed, and shackled at his hands and feet, "people were staring," he said. He was taken into a room. His doctor was not there, and he was seen by a nurse he did not know. Shaun was restrained by the guards and the nurse began a blood draw. One of the guards said to Shaun, "See this baton and this taser? I will fucking taser you." The guard accompanied by a nurse then said, "We'll do one more for good measure,'" getting ready to take another vial of Shaun's blood. The guard then said, "If you are not going to willingly give your DNA, we will take it from your neck." Shaun was not resisting, and he physically could not as he was restrained and still shackled. He was confused as to why the guard escalated the situation, and he did not understand what was happening. Despite his inability to move, he did not consent to the extra blood draw. He did not know what it was for; he asked them to stop and to explain. They said nothing. The nurse took an extra vial of blood from Shaun's neck, which he later learned was mandated DNA collection as part of his registration as a sex offender.

Shaun did not like talking about prison; it was a hard subject, "I want to forget it all," he said. Shaun moved on, talking about what it was like once he was released. He ended up serving three years inside. Shaun had appealed his conviction and got a new lawyer. He wanted to make sure the science of HIV and his viral load was appropriately considered. This time his lawyer was on point. The lawyer had been referred to him via an HIV legal support organization.

On appeal, the Crown prosecutor decided to withdraw proceeding with the case, acknowledging the 2012 legal test put forth by the Supreme Court, meaning that due to having a low viral load and also using condoms Shaun should not have been charged. Shaun felt deeply relieved. While at court, Shaun told me, "I was, like, trying to hold back tears. There was, like, fucking journalists behind me and shit. But you know what's fucking funny? I wasn't even in the newspaper for being let off on appeal. They were there to see if I was going to be convicted. That's why they were there. This attitude, I wasn't in the newspaper for being acquitted. But I guarantee if I was denied the appeal, I would have been in the newspaper. So that's messed up."

The judge said that his DNA sample held in the sex offender registry would be destroyed. Finally, after three years inside, with two years in segregation, he was to be released. He was so relieved. He wondered if he could be compensated for his incarceration now that he was considered not guilty, but his lawyer told him that what happened to him "was the normal course of justice".

Lenore

Sitting in Lenore's yard with her and her boyfriend, she told me about how she came to be incarcerated. She felt her trial was unfair, which she linked to both sexism and racism in her community and within the criminal legal system itself. She told me, "Something that I have learned living in the city is people are extraordinarily racist against Aboriginal women. My prosecutor was racist, she had everything against me . . . the jury was staring at me the entire trial. Part of me was thinking if they were paying attention about what was being said about me, my HIV, or if they were already judging me because of my skin color. It's really opened my eyes to the extent that, 'cause of my skin color, I get treated different. There were no Indigenous people on my jury." She felt she never had a chance and that her trial was a sham.

She was found guilty of aggravated sexual assault and sentenced to two and a half years and was registered as a sex offender for life. A sentence over two years meant she was sent to a federal institution. She was scared to miss her family. She told me, "Now you're found guilty, so they don't listen to you, you're a criminal, no one listened to my questions. I'm just another drunk Indian girl who got raped, no one cares about me." Lenore was referring to how she acquired HIV, which was initially through a sexual assault. Now she was considered the perpetrator, which was a twisted and heinous turn of events for her. "We were expecting community service, and I got a sentence of two and a half years," she said.

Prior to her sentencing, the Crown prosecutor in charge of her case had an expert sex offender psychologist interview Lenore to evaluate her level of risk to the public. Lenore told me it was the first time the psychologist had seen a case involving HIV nondisclosure. They had no official diagnostic tools to calculate her potential level of risk based on the circumstances of the case. She did not fit any of the official criteria of sex offenders that the psychologist used during the interview. Despite this, Lenore was still designated a sex offender, deemed a risk to the public. Lenore told me the psychologist said she was a unique threat and a "different kind of sex offender."

When she entered the federal prison, although health information is supposed to remain private, the guards learned of her HIV status. She told me,

> They treated me like dirt. They called me dirty and were just like "oh we don't want to touch you." In front of me, they would put a couple of layers of gloves on like they are going to catch it from touching me. They really belittled me and made me feel like a disease, really ignorant. . . . They are not supposed to know your charges, but they knew mine. I felt the tension between me and the guards. Like, I had a label on my head, like, you know, an AIDS person. They only touched me with gloves and they used that really heavy alcohol rub after. They talked down to me, like, not talking to me like I was a person.

During her admission into the prison, the guards asked her if she wanted to be "by herself" or in the general population. She asked to be by herself—she was shy and wanted privacy. "I would love to be alone, I need to be alone. I didn't realize that asking to be alone meant what it did." But the conditions and consequences of "being by herself" were not fully explained to Lenore beforehand. In that specific institution, this meant administrative segregation, a euphemism for solitary confinement, which had an institutional requirement to be surveilled under suicide watch. A man guard took her to her room, she continued, "So, they took away my underwear and didn't tell me why. And I was, like, why do you need all my clothes? This isn't safe. I've been molested, this isn't safe. You've got man guards here. No. . . . It took about a half hour before they finally got me to calm down. I have never freaked out that way in my life before. I saw a side of myself that I had never seen before."

Lenore was forced to strip naked by the man guard and placed in a cell with only a concert floor, with a video camera watching her and a window that a man guard would watch her through at all hours. None of her questions were answered, and the guards ignored her concerns. She did not have access to her antianxiety or HIV medications. She hyperventilated and cried. After her panic attack, the man guard gave her a smock to wear, but that did not help. "They had only man guards on duty. My fear of men . . . after what I've been through already. There was no safe position to lay down in those rooms. There is one way, where they can see everything from the window and there is the other way where they can see everything from the camera, no one was explaining anything to me."

After her prosecution, Lenore's case got a lot of media attention, and she was connected with another lawyer. This one was more knowledgeable, and quickly got her released from segregation. In fact, even better, while her appeal was in process, her lawyer got her released back home with her boyfriend. It was during this time that I met Lenore and came to visit her. But things were still unsure, and if her appeal was unsuccessful, it would mean that she may still have to serve the rest of her sentence. She was waiting for a court date to find out. The uncertainty was making her anxious and depressed.

Multiaxial Modes of Suffering

The legacy of settler colonialism, including the ongoing generational effects of the residential school system, means that Indigenous women are asymmetrically affected by the violence of criminalization. Lenore's experience as an Indigenous woman is highly indicative of how structural violence can manifest and be amplified when multiple characteristics compound to increase suffering. She had endured past sexual assaults, living with limited means. She then ended up being charged with aggravated sexual assault and was incarcerated. All the women I interviewed revealed histories of sexual abuse at the hands of men. Yet, those women were the ones charged as sex offenders. Many of the women I spoke with discussed a context where disclosure was highly complex due to their lack of power in the relationships, which was further compounded by racism.

The Canadian prison system is the institutional manifestation of the violence of ongoing colonization. The legacy of settler colonialism, including the ongoing generational effects of the residential school system, means that Indigenous women are disproportionately impacted by the forms of violence that resulted from being criminalized. Around 5 percent of Canadians are Indigenous, but half of the women serving time in federal prisons are Indigenous. Indigenous women spend more time in forms of segregation and have a harder time getting parole. And while the prison population for non-Indigenous people is decreasing in some places, across Canada, the prison population for Indigenous people is increasing as much as 30 percent. Indigenous women are currently the fastest-rising prison population in the country. In provincial jails, the situation can be worse. In Manitoba, a prairie province not far from Lenore, for those incarcerated as minors, 83 percent are young Indigenous women and girls.[4] In this context, the experience of indigeneity and gender along with the mark of criminality result in amplified suffering and material consequences.

In his work "On Suffering and Structural Violence: A View from Below," Paul Farmer asks, "How might we discern the nature of structural violence and explore its contribution to human suffering?"[5] In answering his own question, Farmer also provides answers to Galtung's questions. As a physician and anthropologist, Farmer spent many years in Haiti. He observed that his patients and research informants' lives and choices were highly structured in relation to forms of structural violence—that is, sexism, racism, political violence, and extreme poverty. Haiti as a country has been subjected to multiple intersecting forces leading to extreme levels of suffering, years of political violence due to colonization and the global history of slavery, natural disasters, and multiple epidemics of HIV, tuberculosis, and other parasitic and infectious diseases. In 1991, the Human Suffering Index was developed to measure a range of markers related to human welfare, from life expectancy to political freedom. Haiti was listed as one of the twenty-seven countries globally characterized by "extreme human suffering" representing the only such country in the Western Hemisphere. The three countries fairing worse than Haiti were in the middle of civil wars at the time.

Through an examination of the life histories and untimely deaths of two Haitians, one who died of AIDS and one who was murdered, Farmer connected individual violence and the resulting suffering to structural violence. Farmer wanted to understand what led to increased and compounded vulner-abilities, leading some people to experience more suffering than others due to structural violence. One outcome of Farmer's analysis is the notion of "multiaxial models of suffering," where gender, race, and income play an intersecting and asymmetrical role in rendering individuals and groups vulnerable to suffering.[6] However, Farmer notes that each axis carries limited explanatory power within a silo. This essentially represents an intersectional analysis, first offered by feminist thinkers in the United States in the 1980s, including revolutionary abolitionist Angela Davis.[7] Davis famously notes that the women's liberation movement was run by and for white middle-class women, to the exclusion of Black women, other women of color, and women living in poverty. To understand power and social transformation meant to understand social stratification and how different people have their life chances circumscribed or enabled due to access to racial and class privilege.

Following this form of analysis, Farmer encourages examining human suffering along an axis of gender, race, migrant status, and poverty, concluding that "any distinguishing characteristic, whether social or biological, can serve as a pretext for discrimination, and thus as the cause of suffering." Farmer notes that such a multiaxial analysis must avoid the trap of identity politics, which often obscures forms of structural violence by focusing solely on individuals. Rather, a multiaxial analysis—particularly in the context of this project that also looks at HIV among other diverse characteristics—aims to provide a view from the individual up to the structural level. This can aid courses of action aimed at identifying where to dedicate resources to address and alleviate suffering and understand who is suffering and in what ways.

All the people I interviewed faced a wide range of HIV-related stigma, misinformation, discrimination, and violence at the hands of police and corrections officers and during their court hearings and trials. With a multiaxial analysis, in a context of anti-Black and anti-Indigenous racism, homophobia, and misogyny, intersections of identity and experience resulted in intensified forms of violence.

Black men and gay men who I interviewed faced direct physical violence at the hands of police and corrections officers. Shaun experienced a series of different types of intersecting violence. Violence toward Shaun was enabled, facilitated, and justified because of his experience being transformed by institutions into a criminalized case. Violence against Shaun was intensified due to racialization and anti-Black racism. Much of the violence he described was considered legal and part of sanctioned aspects of being criminalized. In Shaun's instance, legal violence was enacted through incapacitation and the limits on freedom, autonomy, self-determination, and decision-making. His initial denial of bail and his incarceration were all legally sanctioned and put into force via the decision of judges in courtrooms. Yet much of the forms of violence Shaun faced would not normally be considered legal, such as direct physical and psychological violence and assaults underwritten by racism and AIDS stigma, along with the denial of medication and health care—all of which would be considered illegal and officially unsanctioned. Some of the experiences of violence faced by Shaun might be in a liminal area in between, such as the forceful way in which his DNA was taken.

Furthermore, gender, class, and race intersect across multiaxial lines of experience and identity to produce a context of increased precarity and violence for women. Cynthia, a trans migrant sex worker, was sexually assaulted at knifepoint, yet she was the one threatened with charges of aggravated sexual assault. Her experience as a migrant sex worker, who was marginalized due to class and race, meant authorities did not treat their accounts of their sexual assaults seriously. Examining multiaxial modes of suffering underscores that the various forms of violence that result from criminalization are not materially experienced equally. Rather, experiences of violence are amplified and stratified across lines of disparity.

Matteo

Matteo and I made another time to talk on the phone. This time, I called him. I was again sitting in my living room, looking out the window as we spoke. I asked him how school was going. He said he liked getting out of the house; he had been feeling trapped.

Today Matteo wanted to tell me about his time while incarcerated. After the police interrogation, the Crown prosecutor was asking for a ten-year sentence. They argued that Matteo had admitted his crimes. Matteo and his family decided to pay for a lawyer. The lawyer ended up not knowing much about HIV or how to handle the case. Matteo's lawyer counseled him that it would better to plea out, saying that he had no case and would lose if they went to trial. "He said it would be better to say he was guilty of aggravated sexual assault and apologize to the victim and court," said Matteo. Out of fear and feeling broken by the police interrogation, he ended up pleading guilty on a charge of aggravated sexual assault. He was told that if he pled out, he would be sentenced to a lot less time inside prison, two to three years maximum. He feared missing his life, friends, and family. He listened to his lawyer, who ended up getting paid

FIG. 4.1. Matteo's medical request

over $4,000.00 to manage the case. A bill Matteo's parents paid. They did not have a lot of money, so this was a major strain for them and put his parents into debt.

Matteo was transported to prison from a court jailhouse. He was put into protective custody. But he soon found out there was little protection afforded to someone like him. He told me, "I went into the protective custody wing, and there are all kinds of sex offenders there and murderers and everything else like that. And when I got there, they found out my charge. So, they beat the shit out of me. I never fought a day in my life. I have never lifted a hand to anybody . . . I was on an isolated range for violent murderers and would still get harassed. You know, this sexual assault charge and HIV was worse than being a murderer in their eyes." He told me that other prisoners left each other alone, but not him. Matteo explained to me that having HIV combined with what was known as a "dirty charge"—that is, aggravated sexual assault—meant he was marked as the worst of the worst. Despite prison policy, his privacy was not protected, and everyone knew everything.

One day, Matteo was being harassed and pushed around by another prisoner. This was typical. But that day, a guard intervened, which was a rare occurrence. Matteo knew the guard. He was one of the ones who regularly said demeaning things to Matteo. Things about HIV and being gay. "I knew the guard had it out for me," he told me feared the guy. The same guard, a few months earlier, had told a roomful of prisoners that Matteo was HIV positive while they were all getting flu shots.

The altercation with the other prisoner was broken up by the guard. Matteo started to hyperventilate. He was shaken up and started to have what he described as a panic attack. While hyperventilating, the guard escalated the situation.

He was yelling at Matteo to calm down. "I could not calm down with this aggressive guard in his face," he said. The guard forced Matteo onto the cold concrete floor, holding him down with his boot. The guard pushed his boot into Matteo's chest hard, saying, "I don't touch anyone with AIDS." A nurse arrived, and against his consent, stuck a syringe in his arm. Matteo does not know what he was administered, but sedatives and antipsychotic medications are widely used as a chemical restraint in Canadian prisons and jails, making prisoners more docile to control and manage. Matteo lost consciousness and later woke up in his cell. That incident increased his fear of the guard, who continued to harass and intimidate Matteo.

Matteo continued to tell me about the difficulties of being incarcerated and how he was often verbally abused by the guards and prisoners alike. The harassment was more than just words. It impacted his health. Matteo got a bacterial infection. He attributed it to the unsanitary conditions of the prison, telling me how the showers did not drain properly. How the floors were covered in black mold. How the drains and toilets stank. The infection persisted for more than a month, during which time he repeatedly submitted requests to see a doctor. The guards delayed and denied the requests again and again. At one point, the same guard who had pushed his boot into his chest came toward Matteo with his written request to see a doctor. This was the fifth request Matteo had submitted, and he was deeply in pain and concerned. "I really needed to see a doctor," he said. The guard came toward Matteo, looked him in the eyes, and held the request up as he ripped it to pieces and threw it into a rubbish bin.

It was not until the bacterial infection was life-threatening to Matteo that he was finally seen by a doctor. It had become an emergency. Matteo could no longer walk. Despite ongoing harassment and attacks by some, by this point he began to have a few friends on the same range where he was housed. These friends started banging on their cells. One prisoner even lit a fire, in protest so that the guards would take him to see a doctor. There was solidarity when calling out mistreatment by the guards.

Finally, three months after the initial request, he was seen by a doctor. Matteo told the doctor what was happening, how he had been denied access to health care. The doctor was furious with the guards, and she later complained to the prison authorities, telling them that Matteo could have died from the infection.

While incarcerated, Matteo was mandated to participate in the Moderate Intensity National Sex Offender Program, which involved a group of around fifteen other men; many had received sentences for violent sexual assaults, several of them for assaulting children. Matteo had to spend hours sitting with the others, hearing their stories, while being evaluated by a psychologist. Matteo also underwent regular psychiatric evaluation. Those evaluations included phallometric testing, a procedure to determine the sexual preferences of people with penises by measuring their erection responses to visual stimuli depicting various sexual behaviors. Matteo told me, "They put an apparatus on your private parts and make you watch all sorts of rapes, child sex, torture, violence, and see if you are aroused. 'Oh when that guy was getting tortured you got excited.'" Matteo was horrified and angry that he had to undergo such testing. Watching and listening to the videos traumatized him, "I had to go through all that just 'cause I had HIV." The results of the phallometric testing showed that he exhibited the average sexual impulses of a homosexual man. But due to his sentence, he had to continue in the program.

The various psychological test results and his participation in the program contributed to Matteo's overall risk assessment rating, which was used by prison authorities to determine his potential to "reoffend" and fed into policies for how he was to be treated while incarcerated. The higher the rating, the more surveillance and restrictions. The rating would also be used during his parole hearings to help determine if, when, and under what conditions he would be allowed back into the community.

Matteo's assessment ratings were generally good. He had no other offences, and despite being regularly harassed and assaulted, he followed the rules of the institution, and so was generally assessed as having a high potential for reintegration. But one aspect of his rating was not as good. This one was known as the "dynamic factors" rating, which was compiled based on things such as his attitude and level of accountability. The psychologist often marked his attitude as needing improvement. Despite being tested as having normal adult sexual desires, under the logic of the program, the psychologist encouraged Matteo to talk about his own sexual desires as dangerous, as the other participants did. It was hard for Matteo to understand how to participate in the group. The psychologist facilitator made Matteo feel like he had to pathologize his desires just because he was HIV positive. He told me over the phone, "Even the facilitator didn't know why I was in the program. But they had to make a report and rationalize my participation. It was their job. All the normal things I did, because I have HIV, became a thing. But if I didn't have HIV, they would be considered normal behavior."

Matteo found it increasingly challenging and traumatizing to participate in the program, and the facilitator, despite also agreeing that the program was not a proper fit for him, had to evaluate him using the same criteria applied to everyone else. Matteo was described as not accepting the seriousness of his crime. The criteria for the group led to him being perceived as denying and rationalizing his past actions, which was that he had consensual sex while virally uninfectious. One of the activities for the homework component of the program included outlining how to manage deviant sexual urges. He explained,

> When you have this urge to molest someone, how do you then manage that? So, what is my urge? If I ever want to have sex, because I have HIV, what is my urge? I mean, it wouldn't be an urge for anybody else. It is a normal thing, right? But you are supposed to accept accountability, acknowledge that everything you did was wrong, not try to minimize, not try to rationalize, tell them that you are a horrible, horrible person, and what you did was really, really bad and wrong—if you don't go along with that there, then you are not going to get a good report.

Matteo had to explain the kinds of sex he was interested in to the other group members. Using the criteria of the program, Matteo was supposed to describe his sex life as deviant and abnormal. But he resisted; he felt it was homophobic, and this did not go over well with the facilitator. In Matteo's case, he liked anal sex and enjoyed being on top during sexual intercourse with his partners. In the group, Matteo was told by the facilitator that this was "unconventional sex," which meant, according to the group facilitator, that Matteo had issues with power and control. After much reluctance and a series of poor ratings from the facilitator, Matteo eventually gave into the logic of the program—he "had to dig deep inside, bite my tongue, and do what was required of me." Matteo was made to accept the framing of his desires as abnormal despite what he knew to be true about himself and his experience.

Legal and Extralegal Violence

The question asked by Galtung regarding the direct relationship between individual and structural violence is one I wish to reformulate. In my formulation, the question relates to the distinction between legal and extralegal violence. In doing so, I ask the following: Is there a direct relationship between legal violence and extralegal violence? Does one presuppose the other? Using this typology, these questions become crucial, since I seek to examine how legal violence constitutes its extralegal counterpart and how the two are intertwined. For example, illegal violence in the form of an assault can lead to legal violence, as the assaulter, if caught by authorities, will likely be subjected to a form of sanctioned punishment. But can this relationship work in the other direction? Can legal violence result in extralegal violence? And, if so, how does such violence manifest? This constitutive relationship is one I have been invested in to help underline how the violence of criminalization results in ongoing harm.

In the shared experiences of criminalization of those I interviewed, Matteo, Lenore, Cynthia, and Shaun, and those I read about, Angie and Jackson, a constitutive relationship exists through the forms of legal and extralegal violence. Under the colonial and liberal legal regime of

Canada, incarceration is considered legal, as are most formal institutional aspects of the processes of criminalization, pretrial detention or remand, house arrest, release conditions, and sex offender registration. Furthermore, legal public health orders limit some actions and mandate others, constraining and regulating behavior. The practice of administrative segregation or solitary confinement exists in a gray area of legal violence but, in the cases explored in my research, were considered legal.

Under legal violence, the subject of such institutional legal processes is subsequently labeled as a criminal and a threat, and as a result, all the legal forms of violence described by people also resulted in direct personal extralegal violence. For example, one form of legal violence is represented in Matteo's case, when he was institutionally housed in protective custody and later administrative segregation. However, he was mandated to be housed under those conditions because, as he believed, guards leaked his charge of aggravated sexual assault and his HIV-positive status to other prisoners, knowing that violence would be directed at him. This breach of privacy—a form of indirect personal and perhaps psychological violence—combined with the personal physical violence, manifested as multiple assaults, and represented forms of extralegal violence. Those forms of extralegal violence led to intensified legal violence and resulted in the heightened institutional incapacitation of Matteo. Also, Matteo experienced forms of institutional surveillance and control through regulating his movements and abilities, monitoring his sexual partners, and circumscribing his ability to socialize in his community, where he also experienced forms of shunning and harassment via social media.

Matteo's experience recalls that of Cynthia, who was also watched by both the police and her former client-turned-stalker. Like the relationship between extralegal violence and legal violence, two intersecting, interdependent, and co-constitutive forces remain at play—one form of surveillance constituted formally through institutions, and another constituted informally in the social realm. Thus, the multiple and intersecting forms of violence and surveillance are interrelated, where legal violence is co-constituted through extralegal violence.

Two important assumptions underpinning the distinction between legal violence and extralegal violence come to light. The first assumption is that legal violence is society's appropriate response to protect the public, remedy wrongdoing, and incapacitate perpetrators of harm. The second assumption, enacting extralegal violence, should result in proportionate punishment.

The first assumption goes as follows: legal violence is justified to protect persons from extralegal violence. Thus, if someone intentionally enacts an unsanctioned form of violence, such as a physical and psychological assault, they are then incapacitated and punished through legally justified violence. This is the assumption of how punishment is organized in societies predicated under a settler-colonial morality and liberalism.

However, as with many of the experiences shared in this book, the idea that Shaun, Lenore, Matteo, or Cynthia enacted any actual violence remains contested and debatable. Along with the idea of intentional or unintentional forms of violence, typology also comes into play. Despite no intention of harm—or any actual harm—these individuals became constructed as risky perpetrators of harm. Following the common law legal tradition inherited as a product of colonization includes the intention, using *mens rea*—or the notion of the guilty mind. Mens rea is used to prove guilt; if someone had an intention to cause harm, they had a guilty mind. But in these cases, there was there was no discernable intent to do harm. In many cases, Lenore, Shaun, Cynthia, and Matteo each actively worked to mitigate harm through trying to protect their sexual partners with the means they had available, such as with the use of condoms or regularly taking medications, so that they would be rendered noninfectious and unable to transmit the virus. Matteo knew he could not transmit HIV and acted on up-to-date information from his local AIDS support organization. Shaun was undetectable and actively used condoms. Lenore tried to give her partner a condom, but she did not possess the power to force him to use it. Cynthia consistently used condoms with her clients, but that choice was violently taken away from her. These specifics underscore the gendered dimensions at play, where women who engage in sex with men have differential access to the means of protecting themselves from the risk of being criminalized. Conflating those actions with *intent to cause harm* would remain difficult upon hearing the complexity of experiences. So, what does it mean that the criminal legal system enacts legal violence against people when no actual or intentional violence was committed? What does this say about the role of punishment in society and the assumption that extralegal violence begets legal violence?

The other assumption in this distinction between violent actions relates to extralegal violence. This assumption goes as follows: extralegal violence is something that is understood to warrant legal retribution, remedy, and punishment. This assumption is the basic presupposition of the Canadian colonial criminal legal system, which exists to punish individuals for forms of violence not understood as legal.

In the context of the experiences described here, this assumption collapses. Here, the target of extralegal violence also becomes subject of subsequent legal violence. For instance, Cynthia was threatened with criminal charges of sexual assault for her own rape. Matteo was incarcerated under harsher conditions for his own multiple assaults, while Shaun was beaten by the police while in custody and no one was held accountable. The people who enacted that extralegal violence received no punitive consequence; there was no remedy or acknowledgment. This is because the targets of the extralegal violence were all individuals who were not understood as persons worthy of legal protections. Instead, because of their HIV-positive status, criminal charge, and other multiaxial characteristics or race, gender, and sexuality, they became people from whom legally safeguarded persons were protected. The loss of safety and security for Lenore, Shaun, Cynthia, and Shaun become a by-product of criminalization and the undoing of legal personhood.

The assumption that the criminal legal system protects people from unsanctioned violence is here put on its head, as subjects of extralegal violence also then became objects of legal violence. I caution here that I am not advocating for increased state-sanctioned punishment of the people who harmed Shaun, Matteo, and Cynthia. Rather, I question the assumption that the criminal legal system works as a form of justice to remedy personal forms of extralegal violence.

One of the last things Matteo told me on the phone that second time has stayed with me ever since. After his parole was granted, one day during a meeting with his parole officer, her manager joined in on the meeting. The parole officer's manager used to work at the same prison institution in which Matteo had spent three years. She remembered him. She told Matteo that when he came to the institution, the staff had not had a case like his before, and they were not sure how to process him. Matteo told me in a frustrated tone, "She said they didn't think I should be labeled as a sex offender, as I did not fit any of the criteria. But, since I was found guilty, they were institutionally mandated to put me through the program." He was angry that he had to go through the program. It had been emotionally damaging to him, even more so now that he knew even the staff in the institution thought that he should not have gone through the ordeal. Despite Matteo doing no harm, the fact that he was in the system meant the wheels were in motion regardless.

"To Label Someone a Sex Offender, You Know, That's for Life"

For those who come to live criminalized lives, the violence of criminalization extends beyond the walls of the prison and beyond the temporal scope of prison sentences. Criminalized people are cut off from access to certain legal protections and recourse. Criminalization is constituted through colonization and racism. The process of criminalization enables legal discrimination, accompanied by extralegal racialized, gendered, and sexual discrimination that limits criminalized people's ability to access the means to realize their personhood. Criminalization circumscribes access to employment and housing, and the ability to move about freely. People lose their rights to access social and civil life with no legal recourse to secure their own protection.

For prosecuted people, the stigma of their criminal record and sex offender status continues to extend into their daily lives, even after they have served their sentence. For people charged and not yet prosecuted, or who have had charges withdrawn or dropped, the stigma of the charge still lingers. Surveillance permeates all aspects of daily life.

For those who served time and were released, or those who later had their charges withdrawn, working to go back to living their lives and integrating into society after being criminalized was a challenge. Upon release from prison, people told me about how hard life was and how limited supports there were available. Often the supports people felt that they needed to get back on their feet, such as employment support, assistance with gaining financial security, and finding stable housing, were not available.

Shaun

I saw Shaun a second time, this time quickly, outside of a social service agency office he was visiting. It had been about four months since we last spoke. It was now fall, and the leaves were heavy on the trees, many fallen to the concrete sidewalk. We shuffled through them as we walked. I asked Shaun about life after incarceration. He started by telling how he found reintegrating back into the world difficult. "I feel like I have developed posttraumatic stress disorder (PTSD) from the things I experienced while inside," he told me. To manage his mental health, he often isolated himself. He had limited his social world to a small handful of family and old friends. He lived off social support provided from the provincial government, which limited what he could do. He tried finding work, but even though he won on appeal, it was hard with the label of a criminal sex offender hanging over him still. He would work on and off at a factory doing manual labor.

When he did try and participate in society, things did not always work out. For a while, he volunteered at the local AIDS support organization that he went to for services when he was released. Volunteering at that organization provided him with much-needed social interaction and helped him feel like he was integrating back into society.

Later, he started having problems with his landlord and went to the organization for help, asking them to advocate for him. Shaun worried that he would lose his apartment and was upset. After his many years of incarceration, on top of PTSD, he had developed anger management issues. "I do not like this side of myself, but things are frustrating," he said. He was generally calm and soft-spoken but would occasionally have an outburst when he was scared or felt hopeless. "They told me there wasn't anything they could do", Shaun told me he got upset because he felt the staff person was not taking the issue with the landlord seriously. Shaun became angry and raised his voice.

The staff at the organization then claimed that Shaun was acting aggressively, which made him more upset. He felt misunderstood and unsupported. The outburst then caused the staff to accuse Shaun of being threatening, which ran counter to the organization's code of conduct. "The staff person, they feared me from the start, due to my conviction, I could tell," he said. After the incident, Shaun was banned from accessing services and from his volunteer position for two months. "Since I started there, they were freaked out by me, my history and charge, they were just waiting for the right moment to get me out," he told me, still obviously upset, angry, and disappointed.

While he understood that he could come off as angry and was working on it, he also felt he had a lot to be angry about and no outlet to be heard or recognized. He wished others, including those tasked with supporting him, would better understand his needs and perspective. "You know, it's ironic

FIG. 4.2. Shaun's reentering society part 1

that this organization that was supposed to support me acted with the same mindset as the prison," he said, noting that the organization operated with the same logic of the criminal justice system, using punishment and denials of service as a means to an end. Consequently, he no longer participated in

FIG. 4.3. Shaun's reentering society part 2

that organization and lost out on the supports—however minimal and out of touch with his needs that they were.

We continued walking toward the subway so he could travel back to his place. The leaves on the ground made crunching noises under our shoes. Shaun then talked about an incident that took place a month after his release. One day, after working long hours at a factory, Shaun took his dog for a walk at night. A group of men from his neighborhood approached Shaun. One said, "You're HIV positive and you are sharing cigarettes with other people out here. We read about you, you're spreading HIV, that's what the media said." They started telling Shaun that he should leave their neighborhood and started pushing him around. He yelled, "'I'm, like, man, I'm HIV, I'm undetectable, I am no risk, my case was overturned,' and they are like, 'It doesn't matter, you're still HIV positive.'" Regardless, the group of men beat him up, standing above and encircling him, kicking him repeatedly. Shaun was beaten by police, by other prisoners, and now by people in his own community all because of fears associated with the virus and his case. No articles were written about his vindication on appeal. All of which had nothing to do with who he really was or what really happened. Shaun told me that he now often feels unsafe, surveilled, and scared around his home. He no longer goes for walks at night.

This was not the only time Shaun faced physical violence after being released and vindicated. When applying for one apartment, the landlord asked him to come to visit the place. A good sign, Shaun thought. When he showed up, the landlord opened the door and yelled at him, "I don't rent to rapists," and then pushed Shaun down a flight of stairs. Shaun was also denied jobs. After looking for employment for months, he finally found one he thought was the right fit, so he applied. A few days later, he got a message back from the potential employer. The message said his past charge of aggravated sexual assault might make other employees in the office uncomfortable, so despite him having the right expertise, and that his case had been overturned on appeal, they decided not to hire him.

Lenore

Speaking to Shaun that last time reminded me of being back at Lenore's house with her boyfriend. After sitting outside in the garage that day in spring, we decided to move inside; it was starting to get cold as the sun set. While sitting on the couch at her place with her boyfriend, Lenore told me about her life following release from the prison:

> To label someone a sex offender, you know, that's for life, the sentence is over, the three years, but this is until you die. I have to carry this for the rest of my life. I think it's really unfair you know, like it's hard to travel. For jobs, you know, they can find out, and people in your community they know. It's really hard that someone has to carry that for the rest of their life. I'm on the registry that is for rapists and pedophiles. I really don't feel like I belong there. I am on there because of HIV.

She used to volunteer at her son's school in the daycare program but was now no longer able to. "The guidance counsellor that works at my kid's school would love to have me back as a volunteer, but it's the school that won't allow me because of my charge." She told me how she felt as though she was under constant surveillance: "They keep tabs on me, I love working with kids." She felt frustrated and depressed that her charge was keeping her from doing what she loved: "Because of sexual aggravation, they can't have someone like that. But I didn't assault anybody."

Lenore also told me that she worried about many things now that she had been released and that she felt under constant surveillance under her probation restrictions while awaiting her appeal. She told me, "I walked outta prison with even more restrictions than I had when I was inside . . . I feel like I'm not moving forward 'cause I'm still in that box." She continued, "My mum she knows, but she makes like it's a secret, like only family should know. It's embarrassing for the family to have a daughter who's a sex offender. You can't be around kids without supervision, which is hard if I want to spend time with my nieces and nephews."

While out in public in her community, Lenore would regularly face harassment or be denied services. Staff at the local grocery store had also refused to serve her mother. She became increasingly angered and frustrated when explaining it to me. She had served her time and just wanted to move on with her life. She was also worried about seeing her doctor and she no longer trusted health care professionals. Pursuant to a court order, her doctor handed over all her health files to the police and Crown prosecutor, files that were used to help prosecute her as a criminal.

She told me how stressed and fearful she was in her community. She had tried to go to a local AIDS support organization for support, but each time it seemed like they faced difficulties dealing with her. She was frustrated with the limited services available, services that seemed out of touch with what she needed to reintegrate into society.

Despite all of this, she wanted to tell me some good news. Her eyes lit up with excitement, and she smiled. Her boyfriend gripped her hand. She told me that she was pregnant. She was excited about having a new child in her life. I congratulated them both; seeing their joy was heartwarming.

The joy left her face. She looked down, and mentioned how she was also very worried because she had the appeal coming up in a few weeks, and if it was not accepted, she was going to have to return to prison to serve the rest of her sentence. She had close to nine months left to serve, and she was deeply stressed out, upset, and worried. "What's going to happen with the baby?" she feared, as she looked out the window, the setting sun streaming across the window in a red and orange glare.

Death

All the people I spoke with had a very hard time psychologically coping with life under criminalization. As a result of their experiences of criminalization, all the sixteen people I interviewed either tried to commit suicide or had long periods of suicidal ideation. Today, most of the people I spoke with have PTSD, which has a wide range of impacts on their daily lives.

In Canada, one of the primary targets of HIV criminalization are Black men who have migrated to Canada from other countries in Africa or the Caribbean. Due to anti-Black racism, multiaxial power symmetries mean that Black men also face harsher forms of punishment, and bureaucratic obfuscation from prison officials makes many of these people hard to access due to institutional barriers. After incarceration, some people have been deported. In Canada, deportation of migrants has come to be a standard outcome when someone is convicted of a criminal charge that constitutes "serious criminality." Deportation comes to be another added layer of punishment that deepens the material consequences of criminalization, displacing people and potentially placing them in even greater danger for their lives due to differential access to health care and intensified forms of HIV-related discrimination.

Others have died while incarcerated. At its most severe, due to anti-Black racism and HIV discrimination, along with being labeled as a criminal, one's body can be disappeared by the state with impunity. Here, I refer specifically to the lives of Matthews and Williams.

Matthews, a twenty-six-year-old Black man and newcomer to Canada, was convicted of two counts of aggravated sexual assault, one count of assault, and two other minor charges for not telling four women his HIV status before having sex with them. None of those women contracted HIV. He was sentenced to forty months in prison. When he entered prison, his CD4 count, or white blood cells (a measure of the strength of one's immune system), were at 560—a relatively stable number for someone living with HIV. While in prison, he reported a series of health issues to the staff, and in less than a year, his CD4 count fell to 160 and he lost thirty-six pounds. Despite seeing several medical experts, at no time while being imprisoned was he put on any HIV treatments, known as HAART, despite being incarcerated because he allegedly exposed others to HIV. At this time, HAART was widely available across Canada, was covered by provincial healthcare insurance, and was the mandated standard of care for people living with HIV.

Matthews died of AIDS on August 12, 2007, in the Central North Correctional Centre in Penetanguishene,

Ontario, at twenty-seven years old in an era and country where, due to the theoretical access to life-saving medications, dying of AIDS has been increasingly rendered a rare occurrence. There was an inquest into Matthews's death. But in the coroner's inquests into prison deaths in Canada, no one individual can be found culpable and, therefore, no specific individuals were held accountable for his death. The only reason information was released about his cause of death was because prison staff were subpoenaed to testify at the inquest. Otherwise, the prison authorities would not release any information about his death, despite repeated requests from Matthews's family and community organizations. The inquest led to nine recommendations to prevent future deaths, none of which have been implemented by the Ontario Ministry of the Solicitor General. The coroner's report indicated that Matthews died of "natural causes."[8]

Another life disappeared was that of Williams, who, at forty-nine years old, was the first person sentenced after the 2012 Supreme Court's decision. This was the second conviction for the Black father, who was sentenced to four years and nine months, which he served in Warkworth Institution in Ontario. As a Trinidad-born permanent resident, he would be deported after completing his sentence. He pled guilty to charges of aggravated sexual assault. HIV was not transmitted to any of the women involved in this case. At trial, Williams stated he had been lonely since he was diagnosed with HIV in 1996—he was shunned by his family and strangers alike as soon as they learned of his status. As reported by the *Toronto Sun*, he said, "I feel very sorry for them people that I put that fear in them because I'm afraid, I'm afraid to be rejected. It is inhumane," he wept. "It's very cruel," he said to the judge.[9] He also told the court that convicting him and deporting him to Trinidad would be akin to a death sentence, because there he would not receive the health care he needed.

On October 1, 2013, Williams died while in custody. Informal reports from people close to Williams indicated that he had been trying to get medical care for an injury for more than six days before he was found dead due to an untreated abscess on his leg. No details were released from prison authorities, and there was no inquest into his death, as in Ontario, inquests into deaths in custody are no longer mandatory if a death is deemed natural.

All the people who were incarcerated (either as their sentence or on remand pretrial) who I interviewed faced numerous barriers in accessing health care and HIV medications, despite being incarcerated for having HIV. Sometimes people waited months for their medications, and often they had a very difficult time accessing other routine medical supports, such as getting bloodwork to understand their CD4 count and viral suppression. The reality of denying individuals access to health care and medications becomes more troubling when looking at the experiences of Matthews and Williams. In those cases, two Black men, while incarcerated, died untimely deaths in 2007 and 2013, respectively. One was denied access to his life-saving HIV medications, and one was denied access to health care services for an injury. In these instances, lack of action from the system and series of individuals led to their deaths. The outcome of indirect and unintended violence can be equally as deadly as direct and intentional violence.

I do not claim to know what these men lived. Rather, I seek to make it known that the suffering of these men and their subsequent deaths were neither natural nor normal occurrences. Their disappeared bodies were rendered disposable due to being Black, being HIV positive, and having been prosecuted as criminals prosecuted as sex offenders. Their deaths are the ultimate act of privatizing violence, of the disappearing body. I did not know these men, and I did not interview them for this book. They are not able to speak for themselves, and my role is not to speak on their behalf. But from the perspective of research as bearing witness, I hope I am better positioned to deem the experiences faced by men such as Matthews and Williams as unacceptable and seek remedy. I present knowledge of their suffering, of legal and extralegal violence, and the everyday violence experienced by Matthews and Williams, as well as Angie, Jackson, Matteo, Shaun, Lenore, and Cynthia, to denaturalize this violence, to not accept criminalizing violence as normal or natural, not viewed simply as matters of fate.

When Galtung developed his typology of violence, it was imperative to not solely classify forms of violence. He noted, "It is not so important to arrive at anything like *the* definition, or *the* typology—for there are obviously many types of violence. More important is to indicate theoretically significant dimensions of violence that can lead thinking, research, and, potentially, action towards the most important problems."[10]

To be relevant and ethical, a typology of violence is only useful if it can analytically address the problems faced by marginalization and inequality leading to violence in society. Speaking about forms of violence represents one aspect of denaturalizing violence whereas understanding the origins of that violence is another. Examining the relationships between forms of violence can help situate its origins.

Identifying the relationship between direct violence and structural violence, whether that relationship itself is direct or indirect, contributes to a broader critique of the oppressive aspects and practices of public health, the media, the police, and the criminal legal system. Such an approach calls for change.

~ 5 ~

Testimony

Bearing witness is a relational process. Testimony is the act of sharing a personal account of past acts of violence, suffering, and tyranny in a forum where the speech is understood as a form of historical memory. Testimony aims to prevent future tyranny, functioning as cultural memory, and to engage in a politics of atonement.[1] Testimony then aims to make known what others could not know, to prevent past violence from happening again, to call attention as a form of resistance to injustice. The act of testimonial rhetoric is intended to communicate more than the literal meaning of the words. Rather, it is to participate as a conscious action, to share a memory of an experience of violence or political injustice to prevent future instances from ever taking place again.

Bearing witness is not a passive process. Throughout my research process, I kept coming back to the question asked by Sontag, "What does it mean to protest suffering, as distinct from acknowledging it?" This question implicates an ethical role of the observer who bears witness to knowledge related to the suffering of people. Many of the people I interviewed told me directly, in one way or another, "I will speak with you, if you agree to take what I say to people in power to help try and change this situation." My aim in stating this and the role of testimony is not to make some grandiose self-congratulatory claims that I have given voice to people through this book or project. Rather, the people I spoke with gave me purpose and they gave me voice. It was they who empowered me to speak, not the other way around.

Italian philosopher Giorgio Agamben examines a form of testimony based on witness accounts, where the human and inhuman collapse into one another through forms of systemic state violence. Agamben aims to reconsider "ethics in light of the political determination of life worth living."[2] Thus, Agamben contends that testimony represents the act that can bring the human status back to those rendered non-human. The act of speaking testimony becomes an act of claiming one's humanity in the face of the inhumane. However, Agamben sees a problematic paradox and impossibility in bearing witness.[3] In his work on the holocaust, the true witnesses of the violence he studied are dead. The dead cannot speak, they cannot provide testimony, and any witnesses that survived can only act as stand-ins or proxies. Bearing witness then becomes a task of speaking for those who cannot speak and acknowledging the impossibility of witnessing. When asked about the future of prison ethnography at the recent 2017 International Law and Society Conference in Mexico City, feminist and critical criminologist Dawn

Moore contended: "one can't truly do a prison ethnography unless one was a prisoner." While not speaking specifically to the role of bearing witness (and perhaps a contentious sentiment for some ethnographers), Moore, like Agamben, highlights a tension in the impossibility of knowing an experience from the position of an outsider. Can an ethnographic researcher truly speak to conditions inside a prison unless one has lived those conditions? Can a witness to extreme deadly violence speak for the experiences of the dead? These two disparate questions hold within them a similar assumption: unless one has lived experiences first-hand, experiences that may render speaking impossible because people who lived those experiences can be denied voice through death or incarceration, it then becomes impossible to witness and speak testimony. No neat resolutions to these questions or the paradox exist. But this paradox helped me be conscious of my position, which must accompany an acknowledgment of the impossibility of ever truly knowing.

The timing of this project occurred amid a range of policy reform processes held at provincial and federal levels across Canada. Mobilizing the experiences of criminalized people to intervene in these policymaking processes was and is urgent and important. Thus, during the project, I often understood that there was an imperative to share the outcomes of what people had told me about their experiences of criminalization on an ongoing basis. People had shared their stories with me, so that I could take what they told me forward. I shared what I was learning as I was learning it as much as possible, in forums, blogs, public talks, and to policy actors. In so doing, I was part of a movement of social change with many others who were mobilizing acts of testimony and bearing witness to call for an end to criminalizing HIV. The slogan of the movement is *HIV Is Not a Crime.*

It was now the spring of 2019. I had completed my field research. It was sunny outside, and the air had finally begun to have a deeper warmth to it. A group of members from the Canadian Coalition to Reform HIV Criminalization were walking down Sparks Street in Ottawa, Canada's capital. Paved with cobblestones, the street is pedestrian-only and located near the federal parliament government buildings. Our Coalition had formed a few years prior, comprised of people living with HIV, lawyers, workers in the HIV responses, and people who had been criminalized. Bureaucrats were getting lunch on the recently laid-out patio tables lining the street. I was wearing a suit jacket I had bought for the occasion on sale the week prior in a mall in Montreal. As a PhD student, I was broke most the time, living off of small research assistant and teaching contracts. I had not bought new clothes in what seemed like forever and rarely had a need for a suit jacket. But this was one of the rare times.

We were there to testify as witnesses in a government hearing on HIV criminalization for the House of Commons Standing Committee on Justice and Human Rights. The Committee comprises federally elected members of Parliament from all the governing parties and has the power to review and report on the policies, activities, and programs of the Department of Justice, which has the mandate to support the dual roles of the minister of justice and the attorney general of Canada. The Committee also has the power to study policies, programs, and legislation and may review proposed amendments to federal legislation relating to certain aspects of criminal law, family law, human rights law, and the administration of justice.

Beginning on April 4, 2019, the Committee undertook a study on the criminalization of HIV nondisclosure in Canada. I was invited to provide the Committee with outcomes of my research to help inform their study. Among the over thirty witnesses from across Canada, activist Chad Clarke was also invited as an expert witness based on his lived experience of criminalization, as were community-based legal advocates from across the country, sex work activists, and feminist scholars, along with many of my colleagues and comrades from the Coalition.

I was slotted to speak during the same hearing day as other members of the Coalition, including Richard Elliott, a human rights lawyer who used to run the Canadian-based HIV Legal Network. Elliott wrote one of the first policy papers critiquing the use of criminal laws to respond to HIV in 1996.[4] As a leading legal activist, he had now been working to counter this issue for twenty-five years. The movement we were part of had been growing and building. The hearing we were invited to speak at was the result of years of dedicated activism. We were there because of the collective work of many, over many years, who had been working in, against, and beyond the system to counter criminalization.

Late activist and social movement scholar Aziz Choudry underlined that social movements are sites of vital knowledge production and theory building.[5] Choudry's work outlines how the activities and knowledge production of social movements are central for helping to understand and theorize complex social problems. Often it is academics who catch up after the fact. With Choudry's insights, this means understanding the powerful social movement driving change around HIV criminalization is key to also understanding the issue itself. Sociologist Stephen Epstein examined the politics of scientific HIV knowledge in the early days of the crisis and noted how legitimate ways of knowing HIV have always been contested and debated by experts, activists, and people living with the virus.[6] In the context of HIV criminalization, the politics of knowledge has similarly been shaped by a diverse social movement responding to HIV criminalization. This movement included legal advocacy and intervention into specific legal cases, the development of expert and academic evidence, the individual anarchist actions of people living with HIV such as developing guidance to avoid public health surveillance practices, protests to draw attention to the issue in public spaces, the specific targeting of decision makers or media, and coalition building for collaborative advocacy. Activists working to address HIV have helped shape how criminalization is known as an intersectional issue, through a critical race, gender, and sexualities lens and have worked to counter dominant narratives promoted by criminalizing institutions. There has been a range of advocacy and scholarly literature working to "Bring Science to Justice"[7] and to support "science-based law reform" to help courts comprehend scientific knowledge on HIV.[8] This work has been vital in helping to bring the logic of science to the logic of the criminal legal system, even if sometimes the logic of science and punishment do not perfectly align.

In this chapter, I provide some of this insight into the work of the Canadian-based social movement of resistance to HIV criminalization. But first a caveat: while I trace some of these histories of resistance to the criminalization of HIV in Canada my aim is not to reify or commodify the past. Rather, I seek to help create a record of how movements working to counter criminalization developed, to understand the foundation of what came before, to inform ongoing resistance. Sarah Schulman outlined in her account on the history of ACT UP New York that the focus of her book is not nostalgia; it is to help future activists learn from the past to assist organizing in the present. [9] Her work acts as a counternarrative to the dominance of remembering AIDS activists through the lens of individualizing white male heroism. Schulman underlines the stories of those whose lives have been rendered unknowable in AIDS activist history because of racism, poverty, and criminalization. Her work highlights the stark dividing lines that result in white wealthy men being able to stake claims on history, while being careful not to overdetermine identity as a focus of movement politics. Her work is a toolkit for survival in an age where HIV is still not over. Schulman outlines how change can only happen through large-scale movement building and where targets were structural and institutional change, not individual needs or accommodations. I follow this trajectory and approach laid forth by Schulman.

Furthermore, like how critical disability scholars or critical race scholars understand *disability* and *race* as constructions produced through social, political, economic, and cultural relations, so too is *history*. Thus, I acknowledge that the process of telling history is subjective, relational, fluid, and dynamic. I make no allusions to claim that the histories and forms of resistance presented in this chapter are comprehensive or the one universal understanding of these experiences. There will be gaps, as well as varied and differing perspectives. This is one telling, an act of documenting to help inform future work to counter forms of criminalization.

Working In, Against, and Beyond

In 2015, I went on a writer's retreat with my friend and collaborator, harm reduction activist and researcher Zoë Dodd. We invited activists we found inspirational to join us for daytime lunches at the retreat, which was on the Toronto islands, a short ferry ride to downtown. We invited Gary Kinsman, a queer scholar and AIDS and antipoverty activist, who was behind much of the thinking that was foundational to our work and struggle. During our conversation, Kinsman wanted to make room for a range of types of resistance. He highlighted the common tension in activist circles of reformist strategies versus revolutionary strategies, where he noted that our work can target several sites at the same time, through working "in, against and beyond."[10] This approach is inspired by the work of Marxist sociologist and labor scholar John Halloway, who wanted to acknowledge that we are always working within a system, but at the same time, we can create resistance, with an eye to revolutionary transformative change. With this view, in movements, we can conceive of the world outside of the current social order to a vision beyond while chipping away at the violence of the system from in and against. I held onto this ethos of resistance in much of my work after this conversation with Kinsman and Dodd.

It was only in 1989 that Canadian prime minister Brian Mulroney uttered the word "AIDS" for the first time in public. This was seven years after the first death in Canada due to AIDS.[11] The case was reported in the *Canada Diseases Weekly Report*, which detailed the accounts of a Haitian man living in Windsor, Ontario, who had died of a rare pneumonia in February 1982.[12] "Silence thus marked the official responses to epidemic. Silence contributed to it," said Canadian AIDS activist Michael Lynch in memorializing the first ten years of the AIDS crisis.[13] This is the time that Ted Kerr and Alexandra Juhasz now call the "first silence" in the response to AIDS, the years between 1981 and 1987.[14] It is out of the context of institutionalized silence and the insurmountable death toll that an angry and impassioned activist force emerged. Lynch was one of the founders of Toronto's AIDS ACTION NOW!, the direct-action activist group that formed in 1987, the same year well-known group ACT UP (AIDS Coalition to Unleash Power) asserted its presence south of the border in New York City. George Smith, scholar, activist, and member of AIDS ACTION NOW!, underlined that the organization's name must always be written in all caps with an exclamation point at the end; it was always to be a declarative action, as well as an organization.

Using multiple tactics of direct action, advocacy, civil disobedience, community mobilization, capacity building, and education, these groups formed a historic urban social movement focused on the rights of people most affected by the epidemic. By the end of that year, there were fourteen reported cases of AIDS across Canada and four more suspected. Mulroney's statement came after there had been 820 deaths due to AIDS and approximately 40,000 recorded cases of HIV in the country.[15]

In response to the institutionalized silence, future members of the still nascent ACT UP New York formed the artist collective the Silence = Death Project, of whom members would help to form the larger activist art affinity group and ACT UP public relations arm, known as Gran Fury. This group developed the iconic "SILENCE = DEATH" poster, now synonymous with the historic social activist milieu. Using the tactics of advertising and public relations, the posters asserted a voice of anger in public space across New York City. Avram Finkelstein, a member of the collective who developed the iconic political work, stated that their aim was to stake claims on "authoritative space" and to appropriate the use of ever-present urban advertising vernacular.[16] In this context, authoritative space can be understood as both the material space of the city and the political discursive space of policymaking, institutional decision-making, and media punditry. It has been the work of AIDS activists to reclaim authoritative space and to speak back to systems of oppression with our own authority, our own knowledge and experience, our own voices, to speak as acts of reclamation and refusal.

One of the primary concerns of movements of people living with HIV has been to make appeals to rights, personhood, humanity, and life. Tim McCaskell, a founding member of AIDS ACTION NOW!, notes that one of the legacies of the direct-action organization's early work in the 1980s and 1990s was in creating a space for the identity of a person *living* with HIV, as opposed to dying with HIV.[17] A focus on dying was how people had been socially and politically marked by government and medical institutions and various forms of media hype and misinformation in the early days of the epidemic. McCaskell stated that creating the subjectivity of a person *living* with HIV helped to formulate an identity that was outside of the solely homosexual milieu to further amplify the collective voices of HIV-positive people. Celeste Watkins-Hayes's sociological work with women living with HIV in the United States underscores the importance of this analysis, with the viewpoint changing from "dying from" to "living with" the virus.[18] Such appeals to life can be interpreted as one of appeals to personhood seeking for people living with HIV to be conceived of and understood as equal to others and as worthy of receiving dignity in life.

In 2011, my friend Jessica Whitbread, a community organizer among women living with HIV, and I started the AIDS ACTION NOW! PosterVirus project. We wanted to counter dominant narratives and public health framings of HIV. We saw ourselves being framed solely as risks to be avoided and managed, not people to considered and understood. Toronto-based queer artist Daryl Vocat made a poster for the project that year, with the slogan: *We are not criminals*. The poster was plastered across the city as part of our campaign. There was concern after that the poster might reinforce responsibility politics, that certain people deserved to be labeled with criminality over others, and that perhaps dispensing with the label of criminal for all was the way forward. Regardless, the poster made this debate possible and got people thinking about HIV criminalization.

The next year, the project launched a poster designed by queer artist and academic Ryan Conrad, in response the 2012 Supreme Court decision that underlined and reinforced Canada's approach to criminalizing HIV. In response to the decision, Conrad's poster had the slogan: *Fuck the Supreme Court!* The posters were released with a statement: "We are under pressure. Our viral loads are overloaded. The response to AIDS is becoming destabilized . . . The law is creeping further and further in. Our bodies are overmedicalized. And our lives are under-supported. We are not the *public* that 'Public Health' cares about."

In 2012, the Canadian-based HIV Legal Network released a film from director Allison Duke, addressing the complexities of HIV criminalization for women, titled *Positive Women: Exposing Injustice*, which underscores what is it like to live with the constant fear of prosecution and why this needs to change for people living with HIV in Canada. The video featured powerful women living with HIV activists Claudia Medina, Marvelous Muchenje, and Jessica Whitbread. During the film, there is also a conversation with a woman living with HIV whose case went all the way to the Supreme Court and formed part of the 2012 decision. She speaks about being assaulted by her ex-boyfriend and discusses the ways that the context of HIV criminalization can intensify intimate partner violence toward women living with HIV. The documentary, a powerful public education tool, allowed for the voices of women living with HIV to be widely shared, identifying concerns of being oversurveilled, yet underprotected.

Also in 2012, an online zine circulated, titled *How to Have Sex in a Police State: One Approach*.[19] Referencing the title of *How to Have Sex in an Epidemic: One Approach*, the legendary 1983 self-published pamphlet originating safer sex practices and community care came from U.S. activists Richard Berkowitz, Michael Callen, and Doctor Joseph Sonnabend. This new Canadian iteration stated, "Thirty-years after the publication of *How to Have Sex in an Epidemic* we face a new type of emergency here in Canada. State neglect in the response supporting people with HIV is now coupled with intensified forms of state control, surveillance, and criminalization. Canada is among the most punitive countries in the world for HIV-positive people, where the state is turning towards criminalization instead of public education and support."

The website zine has sections titled "Take the Test Risk Arrest" and "How to Keep Yourself Off The Public Health Record," which note that the "less information the state has on you the harder it will be for them to develop a criminal or public health case against you," encouraging people to avoid all HIV or sexually transmitted infection tests at clinics where their real name is recorded. It further states,

> We know that disclosure can result in violence or other consequences. In this case there are still things that you can do to protect yourself and your partners. If condom use is possible, some people will make sure to keep used

condoms from past partners labeled and frozen in the freezer as evidence that the sex they had was protected. These are ridiculous measures, but these are ridiculous times.

There are opportunities for change if people start taking action now! As people living with HIV, we know this: We are responsible and we already practice care for the health of our sex partners. Now we must take action to protect ourselves from the violence of the state, the violence of the AIDS Industry, the violence of AIDS-phobia, and the violence of the criminal injustice system. As the carceral system becomes the watermark of our everyday life it is becoming clear that we are not the "public" that public health is interested in protecting. But we can protect ourselves if we work together, support each other, share strategies and push for change.

The next year, at the Annual Conference of the Canadian Association for HIV Research in 2013, in Vancouver, Jessica Whitbread led a protest with AIDS ACTION NOW! Activist resistance at HIV conferences has a legendary historical tradition and underscores the ongoing politics of knowledge and forms of contestation that take place in terms of what counts as legitimate ways of knowing HIV.[20] In 1983, people living with HIV stood in front of medical professionals in Denver, Colorado, and stated, "We condemn attempts to label us as 'victims,' a term which implies defeat, and we are only occasionally 'patients,' a term which implies passivity, helplessness, and dependence upon the care of others. We are 'People With AIDS.'"

In 1989, AIDS ACTION NOW! and ACT UP New York stormed the stage at the Montreal International AIDS Conference to open the conference on behalf of people living with HIV. And at the 1990 International AIDS Conference in San Francisco, activists called out the travel ban against people living with HIV.[21]

That day in 2013, Jessica led other people living with HIV, researchers, and doctors, all standing in solidarity at the annual Canadian national HIV research conference. The protest was calling for members of the Canadian HIV research community to stop acting as paid expert witnesses on the side of Crown prosecutors in HIV nondisclosure trials. Over fifty demonstrators stood behind a sign that said, *"HIV is not a crime. AIDS Profiteering is"* during Dr. Robert Remis's presentation. Dr. Remis was a prominent epidemiologist who was responsible for Ontario's provincial epidemic surveillance and was also a paid expert witness for the Crown prosecutor in many HIV nondisclosure trials, testifying against people living with HIV. His efforts resulted in numerous people being sentenced to prison. Remis was also well known to the HIV community as a contentious figure who had blamed gay men's sex practices for HIV in the early 1990s. To support the conference action against Remis, AIDS ACTION NOW! released a press release, stating,

> AIDS activists have been increasingly angered at the perceived conflict of interest practiced by this scientist and that he financially benefits off the lives of people who are prosecuted in relation to HIV non-disclosure. In one case, Remis' testimony in the pre-trial led to charges being increased from assault to aggravated assault. Remis is also a member of the Canadian Association of HIV Researchers and was an abstract reviewer for the conference's Epidemiology and Public Health Sciences track. Jessica Whitbread of AIDS ACTION NOW! stated, *"We are calling on HIV scientists and doctors to take a moral stand and*

stop perpetrating HIV stigma against those of us living with HIV. If we are to end stigma and HIV criminalization we need to act in our own movement first." The protest was silent and strong with members leaving their seats in the front row to come and join the demonstration. One member of the audience who joined the demonstration stated, *"When I looked back I saw a dense wall of fierce women activists and it gave me the chills to know how powerful they were. Then I got up and joined them."* Another member of the protest said: *"We need to stand for something or else we will compromise for anything."*

Later, in 2013, Montreal AIDS activist, drag queen, and artist Jordan Arseneault released a poster revisioning of SILENCE = DEATH for the PosterVirus project, reconceived as "SILENCE = SEX." The poster was accompanied by a poem that describes the harsh realities of disclosure to sex partners from the perspective of a person with HIV within the current context where not disclosing one's HIV-positive status is a criminal offense, noting "I am biopolitically pegged for a lifetime of awkward moments."

Arseneault, later working with artist Mikiki, started a collaborative performance and community practice initiative called Disclosure Cookbook, where groups of people living with HIV cook a meal together while sharing experiences of disclosure, fear, and rejection. The project continues an ongoing tradition of mutual aid among communities of people living with HIV sharing knowledge and supporting each other in contexts of oppression and neglect.

In 2014, AIDS ACTION NOW! launched a campaign called Think Twice, meant to help the queer community conceive of ways forward to managing potential disclosure complexities outside of relying on the police. "Think twice before you call the cops" was the main slogan of the campaign, which comprised a series of videos online of DJs, club promoters, activists, and journalists, all discussing alternative strategies, to help mitigate calls to police from the queer community. If public perception could be changed, perhaps a reliance on policing could also be undone.

In 2016, AIDS ACTION NOW! struck again, dropping a banner during Toronto's pride parade calling on the Ontario premier to address the harms of HIV criminalization. The banner said, *Premier Wynne: Stop Criminalizing People Living with HIV.* It was the same year that Black Lives Matter famously stopped the parade, calling for racial justice and an end to the police presence in the parade—an action that soon dispersed across the world to other pride parades. Coincidentally, the premier or political leader of the province, Kathleen Wynne, an out lesbian, was stopped by the halting of the parade in front of the banner for over an hour. Ontario was the province with the highest number of HIV-related prosecutions and the largest population of people living with HIV across the country. The premier never looked up at the banner, but it hung there, nonetheless.

During this time, another target of AIDS ACTION NOW! was legal hearings and courts. Activists wearing T-shirts plastered with the simple but effective statement, *HIV-Positive*, protested several trials of people who were being criminalized, as well as the office of the Ontario attorney general with banners saying *Stop the Witch Hunt!*

Also in 2016, a group of Canadian activists participated at the U.S. HIV Is Not a Crime Conference in Alabama. The conference was strategically held in places needing to highlight stigma and injustice. Alabama had a harsh HIV-specific law that U.S. activists wanted to shine a spotlight on. I was at the meeting, and it was there that a group of us formed as a coalition and have since been known as the Canadian Coalition to Reform HIV Criminalization. The U.S. conference was organized every other year by the SERO Project, Positive Women's Network, and the U.S. People Living with HIV Caucus. These groups collectively had been a driving force in terms of pushing an intersectional analysis of HIV criminalization, one aligned with calls for ending mass incarceration, realizing racial and economic justice, and having a vision for prison abolition in view. The conference had been successful in supporting movements across the United States in repealing or modernizing harmful HIV statutes. But in the Canada, things were more challenging. We did not have an explicit HIV-specific law on the books, our movement could not simply work to repeal the charge of aggravated sexual assault from the Criminal Code. Nowhere in the Criminal Code does it say HIV, so we needed to focus on how the law was interpreted. In Canada, trying to change the application of criminal law would come from trying to influence the decisions of a legal case, implementing guidelines preventing prosecutors from pressing charges, or, in a long shot, changing the Criminal Code.

Prior to 2016, there had been a lot of advocacy work countering criminalization in Canada, but it was one-off protests like that of Dr. Remis, or it was piecemeal and driven primarily by lawyers intervening in active legal cases. With a Coalition, we could become more coordinated across the country and would work collaboratively.

When the Coalition formed, the group ensured it was led by people living with HIV, including those who have experienced being criminalized. This was because, in part, at the HIV Is Not a Crime Conference, the group of us from Canada saw a panel of speakers, led by Robert Suttle, who had directly experienced being criminalized, speak powerfully

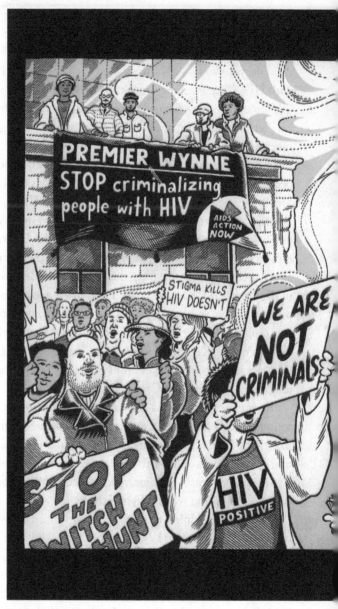

FIG. 5.1. The movement

about the impacts on his life. Suttle was followed by Kerry Thomas, who called in from prison during his unprecedented 30-year sentence, underlining that there were many people who had expertise and insight into the movement for change but could not attend the event due to incarceration. Their voices lit a fire under us.

The same year we formed the Coalition, but after years of pushing from activists, in 2016, the federal attorney general and minister of justice announced on World AIDS Day that the government found that Canada's "overcriminalization of HIV" needed to be reformed.[22] With this announcement, the minister of justice implemented a reform consultation, seeking to investigate ways to undo some of the harms that the past approach had put in place. We saw a path to potential change.

Inspired by the conference in Alabama, to help inform the government's consultation, I gathered stories of incarcerated people, with the help of prisoners' rights groups. Throughout my research, I did not interview people who were currently incarcerated, but as a community, we had access and connections to many people inside prisons. Once collected, whenever we held a demonstration, we read the statements aloud or shared copies with policymakers. One of the stories we read most often was from a man who was near the end of serving his sentence:

> I became involved in a non-disclosure case involving 2 women where a condom was used and my viral load was undetectable, but I was still charged with 2 counts of aggravated sexual assault and was told I'd do 14 years in prison. After four and a half years waiting and in trial, the stigma around my case and its coverage in the media had caused me to be entirely isolated from my community. I

lost my job and my house at the time was vandalized with terrible messages. I was forced to move.

The years on trial and the reaction from the community took its toll on my and I had developed a problem with alcohol, my life became unmanageable and uncertain. My children were not protected from what I was experiencing. They were bullied and ostracized at school, on top of having lost their father from their lives. I am thankful for the healthy relationships we have together and do not think I would be here to communicate this to you without their presence in my life. As part of my prison sentence, I am mandated to participate in sex offender programming—these programs are geared towards people who have done very harmful things to children and women. It makes me feel that my own sexuality is harmful and violent to others. Before all of this happened, I was a happy and healthy family man, who every summer would participate in the AIDS Ride for Life, biking from the coast to Toronto to raise money for people less fortunate than me living with the virus. My future is now uncertain—housing, employment and my family life will all be subject to the stigma of HIV and being a registered sex offender.

The power of stories helped mobilize our movement, bringing humanity to what had previously mostly been legal arguments. When announcing the federal government reform process, the minister of justice noted that the contemporary application of the law was out of touch with current science and the realities of the disease, where HIV is now understood to be a long-term manageable chronic infection and is no longer transmissible when someone is virally suppressed via the ongoing use of HIV medications. We had a meeting with staff of the minister's office for the consultation, and I presented early research outcomes to senior policy advisors from the Department of Justice Canada and the Public Health Agency of Canada alongside a team of others from our Coalition.

During the 2016 government legal reform consultation, members of our Coalition also called for there to be a moratorium on all new criminal cases, with existing cases to be on hold. In Ontario, over 800 people reached out to the provincial attorney general calling for a moratorium. Much of this work was led by Ryan Peck, movement lawyer and head of the HIV Legal Clinic Ontario, and others who were members of the Ontario Working Group on Criminal Law and HIV Exposure, including lawyer Glenn Betteridge and members of Prisoners' AIDS Support Action Network. In Quebec, activists SéroSyndicat held protests calling for one to be put in place as well, led by Jordan Arsenault, who had founded the French language collective focused on HIV justice and health in the province.

In 2017, Montreal, Quebec, was the host of the Annual Conference of the Canadian Association for HIV Research. Many members of the Coalition were there as participants. We wanted the scientists to take HIV criminalization seriously and to help our calls for a moratorium. We pushed the Canadian Association for HIV Research to put out a statement supporting our calls, but it did not happen. So, we mobilized. During a free plenary lunch on the Saturday afternoon of the conferences hosted by a pharmaceutical company, we gathered in the hallway. There was close to thirty of us, with banners saying *Health not prison*, *The law is a bigger risk to us than HIV*, *Stop racist police: End AIDS hysteria*, and *#HIVISNOTACRIME*. We overtook the stage before the pharmaceutical company speaker could get to the podium, but just in time for all the 350 scientists and researchers to be held captive sitting in the banquet hall with plates of food.

Two of our members, Chad Clarke and Michelle Whonnock, took the microphone one after the other, sharing their stories of being criminalized and incarcerated because of HIV. Many people in the crowd had never heard the firsthand perspective of someone criminalized due to HIV nondisclosure before. Clarke and Whonnock were powerful and spoke of what it was like to be in prison, missing their kids, and the challenges of being on the Sex Offender Registry. Despite interrupting the scheduled speaker, they got a standing ovation. A few days later, the conference association issued a statement in support of our call for a moratorium of new charges and a halting of current cases.

As a result of these kinds of actions, the attorney general and minister of justice of Ontario announced in 2018 that the province would stop prosecuting cases where someone had a suppressed viral load for longer than six months and was under regular care of a doctor. A similar response took place in Quebec. Additionally, the minister of justice and attorney general of Canada announced a new federal prosecutorial directive. This directive aimed to bypass the common law precedent legal process. The directive governs federal prosecutors, who handle criminal prosecutions only in Canada's three northern territories. Under the directive, federal prosecutors are no longer able to pursue charges in cases of HIV nondisclosure where a person has maintained a suppressed viral load for more than six months, which was noted as under 200 copies of the virus per milliliter of blood. The directive also ordered those charges of nondisclosure "generally" not be pursued where a person engaged only in oral sex, when condoms were used during sex, or when a person was taking treatment prescribed by their doctor.

The Right to Be Forgotten

In 2018, there was another development. One of the people I had interviewed, who I refer to with the pseudonym Joseph, was continually being declined jobs because potential employers would Google his name and find out about his past charges, even though they had been long dropped by the Crown prosecutor. Joseph would call me and tell me the latest update about how challenging it was to have a past charge of aggravated sexual assault hanging over his head. When his charges were withdrawn after many years, like Shaun's case, no articles were written about Joseph's vindication in court. He wanted to get the articles take down, i.e. de-indexed from being searchable on Google, but was not sure about the way forward.

At the time, there was a vibrant community of activists and lawyers who connected and organized on Facebook working to counter HIV criminalization in Canada. I posted on my Facebook timeline asking if anyone wanted to help, being careful not to disclose too many details online. A lawyer I knew was up for the challenge and willing to take it on *pro bono*. Joseph was eager to be connected to someone who could help. The lawyer and Joseph met, and the lawyer eventually put together a case for the Office of the Privacy Commissioner of Canada, which decided they were interested to hear the case on the grounds of the *right to be forgotten*. This right has the possibility to allow for people to have stories, videos, and photographs of past experiences taken down from the internet. The right was established by the European Union in 2014, which enables people to ask search engines to make certain content unsearchable by looking up the person's name. In Canada, no such right currently exists.

Joseph and his lawyer were asking that Google not index articles about Joseph, so they would be unsearchable, and he could move on with his life. A newspaper article on the case stated, "The case involves the so-called right to be forgotten. An unnamed man complained to the Office of the Privacy Commissioner of Canada over Google search results for his name. He said the prominent results contain outdated and inaccurate information, and they disclose sensitive information. As a result, he has allegedly suffered direct harm, including physical assault and lost employment opportunities and has experienced severe social stigma."[23]

Google fought back with a conglomerate of Canadian media outlets, including the Canadian Broadcasting Corporation, saying they should be exempt from privacy law because the search engine aspect of its company it not a commercial enterprise. The judge did not buy Google's argument. While, as of 2023, the case is ongoing, in an initial hearing, the judge ruled against Google and has allowed the case to go forward in court. The outcome has the potential to acknowledge the *right to be forgotten* in Canadian law and would force Google to de-index the harmful and inaccurate media articles. While much is still to come, this form of legal advocacy has the potential to help undo aspects of the violence of media reporting for all criminalized people in Canada.

Reform?

There were many debates within the Canadian Coalition to Reform HIV Criminalization about the idea of reform.

Would the Coalition push for some changes, only to strengthen the system instead of transforming it? This question was an ongoing tension that arose in our organizing. In examining queer and trans movements, lawyer and activist Dean Spade has raised concerns on the ways movements for reform result in being coopted or how reform efforts can expand systems of oppression instead of transforming those systems. Spade notes that the limited language of rights and equality can result in calls for protections for some at the expense of protections for the most marginalized.[24]

An example of the tension between reform and transformation occurred when I was collecting statements from incarcerated people to share with policymakers at the consultation with the Department of Justice, and later at demonstrations. I got in touch with a support worker at a prisoners' rights organization who had worked with Jackson and several other incarcerated people. I asked them if Jackson and others wanted to submit a statement. I had to wait a few days for the worker to have their regular phone call with Jackson. At this point, he had been incarcerated for almost 10 years, spending most of the time in segregation due to his status as a dangerous offender. It turned out that he was interested in sharing a statement, which the worker transcribed over the phone and emailed to me:

> Being told you must disclose your HIV status to another person is not the same as having the tools or being able to do this in society. It is hard for me to express why as a sub-Saharan man it was difficult for me to tell another person I was HIV positive. I feel like there has been an immense amount of blame placed on my sexuality, without placing any blame on the challenges I face in Canadian society. In public health, we place great

importance on the social determinants of health and how they influence the positive or negative health outcomes for a person. Criminalizing me for my ability to communicate my HIV status leaves out this consideration of social determinants.

Once I collected the statement, it was suggested by some members of the Coalition that we leave out Jackson's name when sending the stories to policymakers. However, our plan had been to add names to the other statements, why leave Jackson's out? It seemed some people working to counter HIV criminalization did not want to engage with Jackson's case. While there had been some pushback from activists in the media at the time of his arrest and subsequent prosecution, since his prosecution, public support for him was limited, as was critique for the harsh handling of the case. As the first, and so far, only person in the world to be prosecuted with first-degree murder due to HIV nondisclosure and transmission, he was considered by some to be blameworthy. He did not fit the innocent victim narrative of some of the other prominent HIV criminalization cases that had been taken up by some HIV activist campaigners. His case brought forth moral complexity. If Jackson had disclosed his HIV-positive status, two women may be alive today. But where was the healthcare system to support those women, and what of the blatant racism and HIV stigma surrounding his case?

If we agreed that HIV is not a crime, as our movement slogan claimed, how could one case be justifiably criminalized while we called for others not to be? Would the Coalition call for an end to criminalization of some while seeing certain prosecutions as justified?

The debate around Jackson's name was not resolved. Our Coalition only works on a consensus basis, meaning that everyone must agree, ensuring there is buy-in on all decisions. The only consensus we could come to was to remove all the names from the statements.

Among prison abolitionists, there are ongoing conversations about how society can support people considered "the dangerous few," such as serial rapists, child predators, and serial murderers, without relying on putting them in cages. Regardless of how I or others might feel about Jackson's case, institutionally his case was constructed as one of the dangerous few. The court had labeled Jackson a dangerous offender, who had the potential to harm people in the future, which is why he is being held in prison indefinitely. The way HIV criminalization has developed to be understood as a sexual assault meant that, as Gayle Rubin has underlined, fears and morality surrounding sex amplify and intensify criminalization, making crimes related to sex and HIV considered the worst of the worst.[25]

The "dangerous few" conversations among abolitionists are oriented around how society can manage the small group of people who may continue to commit violence and social harm when released from being incarcerated, if they were incarcerated at all. How would abolishing prisons contend with these people? How can we just let such people roam free? As leading prison abolitionist Mariame Kaba asserts, when talking convicted serial rapist and former R and B star R. Kelly, "well, surely you don't mean that R. Kelly shouldn't be in prison? We do."[26] Kaba underlines that the pervasiveness of sexual violence in society should signal to us that such violence is not a story of individual monsters. Rather, violent people are a product of a violent society. Kaba argues that the emotional drive to want to punish someone socially deemed a monster for retribution is "mistaking emotional satisfaction for justice" and that "we cannot under any system 'prosecute' our way out of harm."[27] For Kaba, the root cause of the problem is social. Society must be transformed as a way forward to realizing justice.

Critical criminologist Debra Parkes notes that creating dividing lines between the less innocent and more innocent: "legitimates carceral logics and punitive policies by implicitly conceding that there is a durable core of punishable subjects, usually those convicted of 'violent offences.'"[28] Investing in the logic of legal violence as punishment for some (those understood to be the most violent) while claiming that the same violence is an abomination for others, only reinforces a reliance on locking people up as a solution to complex social problems. As noted by Parkes, Ruth Wilson Gilmore has argued that focusing on decarceration efforts on "the relatively innocent" is a flawed approach.[29] Gilmore underscores that institutional violence will not solve interpersonal violence and that a reliance on such will only lead to greater social precarity.

Along the same lines, prison abolitionists, scholars, and activists have called attention to the immense social harm created by prisons as they enact trauma and reinforce disparity, which exacerbates forms of socially understood criminality.[30] Furthermore, there is little consensus on how to define dangerousness—a category that is rife with morality, ableism, racism, and the politics of the day—and measures to predict future so-called dangerous criminality are untested and inaccurate.[31]

Such conversations have also outlined that we must understand what prisons are actually doing, as opposed to what we imagine them to be doing.[32] In Canada, instead of imagining that prisons resolve harm and create justice, this means contending with the overrepresentation of racialized and poor people in prisons and jails, with the overrepresentation of racialized people being institutionally labeled as dangerous, and with the origins of prisons as central to the project of settler colonization.

In thinking through the complexities of reform and the so-called dangerous few, a story I draw inspiration from is that of Jerome Miller. In 1969 in Massachusetts, Miller, a former social worker at Ohio State University became the director of the state's Department of Youth Services. Following media reports and public outcry over abuse and harsh institutional conditions, the former director had been fired and a nationwide search for a replacement was conducted.[33] Despite decades of publicly documented mismanagement and brutality, many youth justice professionals saw the prison model of youth detention facilities to serve a necessary function that was not realized by other means. Miller was hired by the Republican governor at the time as the replacement director. Miller thought differently than other youth justice professionals. He initiated a series of reforms seeking to make the institutions become more humane. But there was internal backlash—the internal staff culture rooted in punishment was inert and not willing to change. Miller quickly realized that the violent system of prison-like youth detention was not going to be saved by reforms.

So, in the early 1970s, Miller led a revolutionary campaign, closing all the youth detention centers across the state, releasing all the young people inside. In doing so, Miller worked closely with nonprofit organizations to create a new system where services were provided in the young people's local communities. With this new system, Miller worked to first release all the youth understood to be the most dangerous. The logic behind doing so was that if social supports could be put into place to create an environment of care and accountability for the young people understood as most violent, this could easily be done for everyone else. The new system worked, saving taxpayer dollars and increasing the life chances of marginalized young people across the state.[34] Once the institutions had been emptied of all the young prisoners, in anticipation of backlash, Miller quickly demolished the old institutions and sold the land.

Miller's story underlines the contextual nature of institutional framings of dangerousness and how working within a system can achieve the goals of working beyond.

Following the debate about Jackson's name, in 2022, the Canadian Coalition to Reform HIV Criminalization had an internal debate over the use of the term "unjust criminalization." The term was widely used in our movement, to describe HIV criminalization, underlining that some forms of criminalization are just while others are not. Some in our group argued we should use the term in public advocacy to refer to an instance of HIV nondisclosure where there was no intent to transmit the virus, meaning that when there was intent to transmit criminalization was justified. To some it may have seemed like minor wordsmithing; to others using the term unjust meant we may be signaling support for forms of criminalization, which was the wrong approach if we were to have a strategic eye to ending criminalization. This minor wordsmithing signaled what we stood for. I sent the following email to our Coalition to oppose the use of the term:

> After examining many cases in detail, as well as meeting many of the people involved, I personally do not feel that any of the outcomes of the cases I've encountered could fall under the classification of "just." I do not believe the Canadian criminal legal system can produce or realize justice. Such a system, rooted in retribution, colonization, and punishment, is incompatible with notions of

justice—which can only truly come through forms of individual, community, and social healing.

Furthermore, as someone with prison abolitionist tendencies, I do not view any form of criminalization to address complex social problems as just (e.g., drugs, abuse, poverty, sex work, assault, or HIV). But I do very much agree that there is a need for forms of intervention and regulation for some of these complex social problems. And we currently only have a very flawed and violent system to provide responses.

To address complex social problems, the current system produces legal outcomes (not justice, or just outcomes). The legal outcomes that are produced through this system involve forms of punishment. Punishments, applied by the state, are a form of violence.

Applying state violence as a solution to address complex social problems (where interpersonal harm or violence may have been involved) is not a means to realize justice or healing and will only create further social and individual harms.

But we can limit the scope and intensity of state violence, and the forms of punishment that result, through certain reforms, such as with what we are working to do with our Coalition. This limiting of intensity of state violence is a good start, but it is not the end of the work that needs to be done to realize a more just society.

Working in, against, and beyond the current system, with pragmatism, and an abolitionist view, is possible as a principled approach to limit the scope of state violence. I can reject the stance that the system produces justice, while working to limit the scope and harms that such a system produces, working within the logic of that system to change it, while also seeing beyond the limits of such a logic.

In the end, the Coalition decided to stop using the term "unjust" publicly, opting for a consensus agreement on the term "discriminatory criminalization." But the assumption still exists among many that some forms of criminalization are warranted, and that the way forward is punishment. Regardless of disagreements with vision, our Coalition was stronger together than apart, and we had been making collective progress.

Although not explicitly stated, the Coalition has been moving forward with what perhaps critical criminologists Nicolas Carrier and Justin Piché might call a "minimalist approach" to penality.[35] This approach acknowledges what activist and movement leader Harsha Walia identifies the debate between reform and revolution can be overly simplistic and reductive, noting that: there can be nonreformist reforms, which do not expand systems of oppression while working to limit harms of policing, criminal legal system, and prison institutions.[36]

The main nonreformist calls for change have been seeking to limit the ways in which criminal law can be applied, so it impacts less and less people over time. In 2022, the Coalition undertook a Canada-wide consultation with people in the HIV movement to help elaborate a platform of action, one that could be used to advocate for change. The outcome includes many nonreformist reforms, including calling to end HIV being understood under the laws of sexual assault; to end the use of the Sex Offender Registry; to end considering HIV nondisclosure an act of "serious criminality," meaning a prosecution would not result in deportation; and a review of past convictions "so that people living with HIV previously criminalized under these harmful and stigmatizing laws no longer have to live with the label of a sex offender and criminal." It is further noted by the

Coalition's platform, "the stigma and harsh sanction of a criminal prosecution and conviction is not justified in cases where someone,

- did not understand how the infection is transmitted;
- disclosed their status to their sexual partner or honestly believed their sexual partner was aware of their status through some other means and voluntarily engaged in sex; took precautions to prevent transmission (e.g. condom use, being on treatment);
- did not disclose their status, or did not take or insist on precautions, because they feared violence or other serious negative consequences would result from doing so;
- was forced or coerced into sex; or
- did not intend to transmit the infection." [37]

For me, the notion that intent to transmit HIV should be regarded as a crime is a trade-off of working inside a system that had a legal precedent of many criminal prosecutions. No one I had met during my interviews, nor any cases on which I conducted archival research, fit into these criteria of aiming to transmit HIV to someone else on purpose, where transmission has also taken place. Working to limit the law's scope to only the hypothetical instance of intentional transmission was potentially one path forward to limit the scope of criminalization. I did, however, know many people, both incarcerated and who had been released and were on the Sex Offender Registry, who may be vindicated if the government listened to our calls for change.

However, there has been much debate about this approach. The Coalition comprises a range of people with different outlooks on the legal system and different long-term game plans seeking to find common ground to collectively call for limiting the scope of criminalization and the harm that results. Some people living with HIV, activists, and community organizations felt the Coalition was not going far enough and should consistently call for the all-out decriminalization of HIV nondisclosure. Would such a reform lead to reinforcing the idea that acquiring HIV is the same as bodily harm from an assault? If HIV is a normal and common human experience in the current treatment context, should acquiring HIV be equated with any form of bodily or psychological harm? As the experiences of those in this book tell us, the harms surrounding HIV, which are enacted by police, in courts, by prisons, and in the media, are a result of how HIV is socially understood (re: stigma and discrimination) or are about lack of access to treatment and medical care. These harms pertain to social inequities more so than to the biomedical impact of the virus itself. In the end, HIV is not the concern, but society's response to those of us with the virus is.

Like this, a nonreformist reform approach was continually negotiated. Much more work would need to be done.

Testimony

Let's turn back to that spring day in 2019, when members of the Coalition testified to a panel of politicians from across the political spectrum. Before coming into the committee room, I had a debate with myself about sharing my own HIV-positive status when presenting. For me, living with HIV and doing this research perhaps gave me insights into the work and issues. I felt I had an ethics of care on the topic that others may not. For me, my subjective position strengthened the work. However, at the same time, I did not want a perception that I was focusing on myself. Nor did I want to open myself to criticisms from politicians that my research was not objective, or that the findings were biased. As a qualitative researcher, trained in feminist approaches and critical social science, I understand all research to be biased and subjective, and claiming those positions is what enables robust research to take place. But still, notions of objectivity are pervasive and used to discredit researchers. Despite living with HIV since I was a teenager, there was also something vulnerable about the idea of sharing my HIV-positive status in this context as a witness. There was a nagging insecurity within me that as someone living with HIV, I would not be taken seriously.

So often we do not know the motivations behind why researchers study what they study. For me, there was more on the line. But I did not want to detract from the findings and so decided to let the research stand for itself. Plus, if anyone looked me up online, they could likely find the information quite quickly. Still, in the context of presenting my research on the harms of HIV nondisclosure criminalization, I ended up negotiating my own disclosure. The odd irony and unendingness of disclosure dilemmas were not lost on me.

The committee room we were in had recently held a high-profile televised public hearing on another issue. Contentious witness testimony from the leather chairs where we were to sit had been on the evening news for a week prior. While our hearing was much lower key with no cameras in sight, being there in person amplified the stakes of it all. The room was wood-paneled, and large rectangle lights flooded us from above. I sat down in the chair, my new suit jacket crumpled. I put my notes down on the mahogany table in front of the microphone, behind a card printed with my last name. I remembered all the people I spoke with across the country over the previous years who had shared their experiences. I focused on not crying. This was my testimony:

Thank you to the Chair and the members of the justice committee.

I'm currently a doctoral student at Concordia University. Later this year, I'll begin a Social Science and Humanities Research Council Banting postdoctoral fellowship in the department of criminology at the University of Ottawa. I'm also a member of the Canadian Coalition to Reform HIV Criminalization.

For my doctoral research, I was funded by the Canadian Institutes of Health Research and Concordia University to examine the experiences of people living with HIV across Canada who have been charged, prosecuted or threatened criminally in relation to alleged HIV non-disclosure. To my knowledge, this is the first qualitative research study, globally, that is focused specifically on HIV criminalization from the perspectives of the people who have lived it.

Today I'll share findings from that study. I've also provided to the committee clerk statements about the experiences of the harms of criminalization from the people who are currently incarcerated.

In speaking directly with people who have been criminally charged, my research calls into question dominant understandings of the courts and media that people living with HIV are violent perpetrators who are actively trying to transmit to others. Rather, what comes to be institutionally understood as wrongdoing is much less obviously so. Because of criminalization, complex and nuanced situations—including people's silence, fear, actual disclosure or in some cases their inability to address their own HIV status—is forced by the criminal justice system into a dichotomous narrative of victim and perpetrator.

I conducted 28 interviews with 16 people from five different provinces. I spoke with five women and 11 men. One of the women identified as a transwoman. This was a diverse group of people who comprise a wide range of experiences across the spectrum of people who are facing criminal charges in relation to HIV non-disclosure. Many of them are socially marginalized, including Black and Indigenous people, gay men, people who live in poverty and women with histories of street-based sex work. The youngest person I interviewed was in their mid-teens at the time of charges and the oldest was in their mid-fifties.

The interviews consisted of detailed questions about people's experiences from the time they found out they were criminally charged, to, if relevant, their arrest, court proceedings, sentencing, incarceration, release and their lives outside after their sentence. Three of these people had been threatened with criminal charges by police, while 13 had been formally criminally charged—all with aggravated sexual assault. HIV transmission was alleged to have taken place in only one of these cases.

All of the women I interviewed indicated having long histories of sexual abuse by men and discussed a context where disclosure was highly complex due to their lack of power in the relationships. A woman I spoke with was charged with aggravated sexual assault because she had been gang-raped and did not disclose to her rapists. Another woman who was threatened with criminal charges was raped at knifepoint, yet she was the one threatened with charges of aggravated sexual assault. Both had histories of sex work and authorities did not treat their accounts of their sexual assaults seriously. One of these women told me that if she's guilty of anything, she's guilty of being raped.

The charge of aggravated sexual assault was extremely confusing for people because they understood that the sex they had was consensual—outside of those two instances. A majority of the people in the study were concerned about transmitting HIV to someone else. They understood that they acted in a manner so as to protect their partners from potential transmission, such as noting that they took their medications regularly, rendering them uninfectious, or that they used condoms, or both. One woman I spoke with handed her partner a condom prior to sex, which he did not use. She is now a registered sex offender. In some cases, people had disclosed to their partners who later went to police and lied about the disclosure having taken place.

Due to being charged with a criminal sanction usually reserved for the most violent, non-consensual, actual sexual assaults, combined with being HIV positive, the people I spoke with were confronted with intensified forms of punishment, violence and discrimination. This included denial of bail and ultimately incarceration for long periods of time on remand prior to trial or before charges were dropped or stayed, extraordinary release conditions as part of bail, or conditional release that included being mandated to present oneself to police 24 hours in advance of proposed sex with their sexual partner and having the partner consent to sex in front of police. The people I interviewed who had these conditions imposed had undetectable viral loads.

Additionally, people I spoke with told me that there was a widespread lack of knowledge of the current science of HIV by police, lawyers and courts. This put people who were criminally charged in the position of having to educate those tasked with criminalizing them about viral load and transmission. People felt that the police's stigma and ignorance was enabled by the legal context of criminalization.

All but two of the 14 people charged indicated that this was their first-ever criminal charge. Despite this, all but one of them were denied bail due to the perceived severity of the case and were either held in remand or under house arrest for long periods.

Seven people I spoke with were prosecuted, with five of the seven pleading guilty. The reasons they indicated for taking a plea were the following: having been coerced by their lawyer into pleading despite having undetectable viral loads or having used condoms; being fearful of missing their families; or being ashamed of the charge and of having their HIV status exposed to the public. The longest sentence served was close to 15 years. The shortest sentence served was approximately two and a half years.

From the point of arrest through trial, incarceration and release, people I spoke with described a series of events that were marked by HIV-related stigma, panic, discrimination and fear. People described a range of forms of violence at the hands of government employees, namely police officers and prison staff. These included denial of health care and medication access from corrections employees. One person I spoke with almost died because guards would continually rip up his urgent requests to see a doctor in his face.

Other forms of violence included long periods of incarceration and administrative segregation as well as breaches of privacy wherein corrections officers would disclose their HIV status and charges in front of others, knowing that physical violence would or could result.

Additionally, there were assaults by police officers and corrections officers accompanied by stigmatizing comments and discriminatory behaviour. One man told me:

I was getting beaten by all the inmates because their corrections officers had disclosed my charge to people on the range. I was on an isolated range for violent murderers and would still get harassed. You know this rape charge and HIV was worse than being a murderer in their eyes. One officer pushed me to the ground naked holding me with a boot to my chest saying he would never touch a man with AIDS.

Another indigenous woman told me, "They treated me like dirt. They only touched me with gloves and would use really heavy alcohol rub afterwards. They talked down to me like I was a non-person, an AIDS person."

Given the charge of aggravated sexual assault and the resulting registration as a sex offender, people were not able to get employment in areas where they had past experience and expertise. They were denied jobs when applying. Many were on social assistance, even though they wanted to work.

People were regularly denied housing. One person was told, "We don't rent to rapists." The person had had their charges dropped by the crown but information about their case was widely available online.

All of the participants noted that they failed or did not meet the criteria of the various psychological tests to determine what kind of sex offender they were. A few noted that the tests themselves had caused ongoing psychological trauma. This was due to being forced to watch videos of child pornography and violent sexual assaults, as well as being coerced into defining their normal adult sexual desires as deviant or wrong, just because they had HIV.

The past charge continued to extend into their daily lives by threatening their economic security. One indigenous woman told me, "I'm not allowed to work in the school I used to. I love working with kids, but now the school won't allow me to." One person told me, "To label someone as a sex offender, that's for life. I have to carry this for the rest of my life. I think that's unfair."

All of the people I spoke with had a very hard time psychologically coping with being understood as a violent rapist. As a result of their experiences of criminalization, all had either tried to commit suicide or had long periods of suicidal ideation. Today, a majority of the people I spoke with live with post-traumatic stress disorder, which has a wide range of impacts on their daily lives.

Through speaking with criminalized people directly, it becomes apparent that applying the criminal law, specifically the laws of sexual assault, causes greater harm, often exacerbating situations that are already marked by stigma, trauma, shame and discrimination.

Thank you[38]

After the hearing, I felt relieved. The sun was still shining in an almost golden hour glow. The bureaucrats had dispersed; there were less people on the street. The group of us who had testified went for a late lunch on a patio on Sparks Street.

Two months after our testimony on that spring day, the House of Commons Standing Committee on Justice and

Human Rights released a report on their findings from the hearings. The report referenced all our statements, and there was a recommendation to immediately stop applying the laws of sexual assault to cases of HIV nondisclosure. This was a small success. The Committee understood the harms of using aggravated sexual assault and the Sex Offender Registry. While the recommendation had no force behind it, this was a small step forward that gave a mandate to the minister of justice to push for change.

Activists continue to call for further reform and transformation, and the fight to change how laws are applied in cases of HIV nondisclosure across Canada continues. In the end, for me, the slogan *HIV Is Not a Crime* rings true. But in a country where there are years of a common law legal precedent stating otherwise, where people are still facing charges, are still incarcerated, and still on the Sex Offender Registry, how do we move forward to mitigate the harms of the current system while striving toward the beyond?

In 2021, in seeking to answer such questions, members of the Coalition held a gathering with Indigenous HIV leaders and organizations to conceive of restorative justice and community-based alternatives to HIV nondisclosure criminalization, particularly through the lens of people experiencing gender-based violence. The conversation is ongoing; this movement will continue to bear witness to the harms of criminalization and collectively will keep calling for change in, against, and beyond.

$\sim$ 6 $\sim$

Conclusion

It was the summer of 2022. I was at home watching the evening news when I got a message via Facebook Messenger. It was dusk outside. The sun had just set. I had stayed in touch with many of the people from my project; we would regularly check in on each other, sometimes I would help connect people to supports. Several people were also actively engaged as activists, and we would update each other on advocacy developments. Although, like everything else, COVID-19 had massively hampered any progress we had made around HIV criminalization reform.

This message was from Matteo; I had not heard from him in a while. A long message popped up as the notification dinged on my phone. He was stressed. He had an arrest warrant out on him for not going to his annual sex offender registration check-in at the police station. His PTSD was spiking. He told me he had been in denial about still being on the registry and could not bear to deal with it anymore. He felt he had done everything he could do, when the minister of justice launched the calls for reform his wishful thinking took over, and he was exacerbated and wanted his ordeal to be done with. I felt terrible. "We need to get you a better lawyer," I said. He replied, "I can't do this again, if they arrest me, I might as well be dead."

Daily Lives of Violence

My research began with a single question: What are the daily experiences of HIV-positive people who have been engaged in the criminal legal system because they allegedly did not tell their sexual partner(s) that they are HIV positive? After years of research, the answer to that question is that people's daily experiences are mediated by violence. Through the process of criminalization, under the logic of authoritative and expert institutions, complex experiences are dichotomized, rendered into legal facts, and used to deconstitute personhood. In my analysis, I have outlined how undoing personhood via criminalization is a form of legal violence that leads to other forms of extralegal violence. When we listen to the experiences of criminalized people, there is a massive disjuncture between how such people understand their own lives, as opposed to how they come to be known through the logics of institutions.

The material outcomes of criminalization extend beyond formal institutional punishments into a broad range of populist forms of violent retribution, social marginalization, and discrimination. Criminalization reaches beyond the bounds of the criminal legal system to permeate every aspect of someone's daily life, circumscribing their behavior and constraining life chances.

A society predicated on punishment as the primary avenue to address social problems will result in the proliferation of the logic of punishment driving the actions of institutions outside of the criminal legal system. This logic of justified punishment disperses and intervenes in all ways of thinking and doing. Here we see health care workers, public health practitioners, community members, HIV and AIDS organization support workers, and the media all acting like police, hence as further arms of the criminal legal system.

Criminalization denied people's access to a central aspect of personhood—they were cut off from the social contract of life in a liberal society. They lost access to privacy related to their sex lives and health status. They lost access to freedom. They lost the ability to speak about their own experiences and to be heard and understood. No longer considered a person worthy of protection, people lost access to physical and emotional safety and security. They all experienced stigma and discrimination based on who they were as people. Being classified as perpetrators meant they were denied the rights of personhood.

The suspension of any rights to personhood for the risky, guilty, and criminal is justified by the contention that it upholds the rights and protections of the innocent and victimized. The alleged victim is granted access to civil life as a protected person, while the criminal must live in precarity and is rendered civilly and socially dead. This criminalization process is completed through liberal legal processes, underwritten by the legacy of colonization, which position certain groups as legal persons and guarantee them the rights of personhood, while positioning others outside of legally safeguarded personhood.

While criminalization may be universalizing for people living with HIV, its impacts are socially stratified across dividing lines of racialization, gender, citizenship, and sexuality. The lived experiences of common human behavior, such as informed health care decisions, problems or misunderstandings, disputes or lies, moments of silence, and things unsaid or no action at all came to be framed not by the people originally involved but instead via institutional actors and authorities underwritten by colonial racist, sexist, and homophobic logics.

All the women interviewed indicated having long histories of sexual abuse by men and discussed a context where disclosure was highly complex due to their lack of power in the relationships. Several women I spoke with were either active sex workers or had histories of sex work. Four of the five women I spoke with were women of color, and three were Indigenous. Their experiences reveal the ways in which the criminalization of people with HIV continues to be racialized and gendered. The legacy of settler colonialism, including the ongoing generational effects of the residential school system, means that Indigenous women are asymmetrically impacted by the forms of violence that resulted from being criminalized.

Five of the men I interviewed identified as gay. During interviews, they told me how they felt that their charges were brought about by homophobic stigma and discrimination. A few of these men had release conditions banning them from using gay social media and hook-up apps, along with conditions banning them from going to gay communities in their cities or towns.

Due to multiaxial intersections of experience and identity, the racialized and queer people I spoke with experienced intensified legal and extralegal violence.

THE PUBLIC HEALTH POLICE

Many of the people I spoke with also had been subjects of public health orders under various provincial public health acts. The orders put constraints on people's behavior in ways like criminal legal sanctions, such as with bail or parole conditions. The orders often mandated counseling, which for many felt pathologizing and disconnected from people's realities. Under the orders, there were legal requirements to take medications regularly (when people were already virally suppressed and were already taking the medications for their own health and for prevention) and other odd conditions or unnecessary practices, such as using condoms for oral sex, a practice unnecessary when an individual is virally undetectable, or a requirement to put on condoms prior to having an erection (which is almost physically impossible). People told me they felt the actions of public health authorities were often out of sync with their actual behaviors and driven by outdated and stigmatizing, fear-based ideas stuck in the past of AIDS that had not caught up to current social and scientific realities.

All of the gay men I spoke with were mandated either through public health orders or as part of bail or parole conditions to attend mandatory counseling to promote disclosure. These men had already learned about HIV and sexual health from a local AIDS organization, information they used with their partners. The mandated public health counseling was different from what they learned from AIDS organizations and made them feel pathologized and bad.

They felt the mandated public health counseling approach was driven by homophobic fears of gay sex. Furthermore, as a result, they no longer trusted many health care workers and felt scared to talk to them truthfully about their sex lives. All people interviewed noted that they had lost trust in health care providers and public health authorities. They now equated public health and health care workers as just another part of the criminal legal system.

Many had their health records subpoenaed, and some had their own doctors testify against them in court. People now no longer felt safe being honest with any health care worker for fear of information being used against them in the future.

These findings also reveal how the violence of criminalization is not solely a result of punishment under the criminal legal system but comes in the form of surveillance, control, discrimination, and from a range of other institutions such as public health authorities. Criminal laws and public health laws intersect and reinforce one another. Information from health care workers can be used within the criminal legal system for the purposes of criminalization.

CRIMINAL LEGAL SYSTEM

All the people I interviewed had also lost any faith in the criminal legal system. None of the people I spoke with understood that the acts they engaged in were violent, and all felt the consequences were massively disproportionate and now feel as though they have been victimized by a broken system. Despite being charged and prosecuted in relation to HIV nondisclosure, they received no such supports around disclosure through the process of engagement with the criminal justice system, and some felt even less equipped to deal with their HIV-positive status due to now also being labeled a criminal. Overall, all the people I spoke with described a severe lack of trust and dismay at the Canadian criminal legal system because of their experience.

Many of the people with whom I spoke had a difficult time accessing legal counsel who had an adequate understanding of HIV criminalization. In some cases, people paid for lawyers, and in other cases, people had access to legal aid. A majority of the interviewed came from working-class backgrounds, and therefore the high cost of hiring lawyers was an issue. In many instances, people noted that they felt as though their legal counsel was ill-informed on the science of HIV transmission. Some thought that their lawyer accepted the idea that their clients were dangerous perpetrators, and as a result, people felt that they had been pressured to accept guilty pleas. It was noted, however, that duty counsel and legal aid lawyers were better informed than lawyers that people paid for, but people felt that the publicly funded practitioners had limited time to support their cases in the ways people wanted.

Many of those charged had no prior criminal history yet were denied bail and immediately incarcerated for long periods of time before their trials, if a trial occurred. Eight people I spoke with were prosecuted, with five of them pleading guilty. The reasons indicated for taking a plea were because they felt coerced by their lawyer (despite having undetectable viral loads or having used condoms), were fearful of missing their families, or were ashamed of the charge and of their HIV-positive status being exposed widely to the public. None felt they were guilty of a crime deserving of such a harsh response. The longest sentence served was close to fifteen years, while the shortest sentence served was approximately two and a half years. All but two indicated that they were virally undetectable when the incident that led to the charges took place.

THE VIOLENCE OF MEDIA

Many of the people interviewed faced sensationalistic media coverage labeling them as violent predators who were a threat to the public. This media coverage acted in concert with policing and court framings of criminalized people's cases. Often media articles published false information, such as stating that people had been intentionally trying to infect others with HIV. In the age of the internet, negative media articles are now available forever. This fact had multiple negative impacts on people's lives, including people socially isolating themselves due to stigma, shame, and discrimination.

Media representations can lead to direct personal forms of violence in the lives of those criminalized. People lost access to privacy when information, such as police press releases and sensationalized media reports that include private photographs, were spread widely. Private details about people become public spectacle, and those individuals become recognizable in their own communities. Social media and online posts disclose information and charges. Such information can be dispersed and mobilized to discriminate, to enhance surveillance. Those criminalized were shunned and banished from public spaces and services, as well as denied housing and employment, and they face a wide range of physically and emotionally violent consequences such as beatings and verbal abuse. Due to the violence of media reporting, and the stigma surrounding perceptions of their cases, criminalized people had limited access to privacy and safety in their communities.

Most of the people I interviewed discussed the important role that community-based HIV and support organizations played in helping them through the difficult process of being criminalized. Some people were connected to groups providing support to incarcerated people while they were inside prison, support they often regarded as lifesaving. For people who served time and were released, or those who later had their charges withdrawn, working to go back to living their lives and integrate into society after being criminalized was a challenge. Upon release from prison, people talked about how hard life was and how limited support there was available. Often the supports people knew they needed to get back on their feet, such as employment support, assistance with gaining financial security, and finding stable housing, were not available.

Some also felt that the label "sex offender" was intimidating and threatening to people in their local HIV and AIDS organizations. The frustration with lack of supports, coupled with people's PTSD from being criminalized, led to instances of conflict within organizations. In some cases, such conflicts resulted in people being barred from accessing supports. The experience of being barred from support organizations after release from incarceration happened to three of the individuals who were interviewed. These individuals lost trust in community organizations and made them feel shunned and shamed. They also felt that if they went back and "slipped up" again, the organizations might call the police.

The people I interviewed hoped for more holistic supports and workers who understood the complexities they faced, such as the mental health issues and managing anger after being incarcerated. Instead of being supported, they were met with the same punitive reactions enacted by the criminal legal system that had banned, shunned, and shamed them.

A Criminology of the Criminalized

I came to studying this issue from an activist point of view, as someone living with HIV and as someone who wanted to develop knowledge to help undo the violence of HIV criminalization. I spent a long time reflecting, as both an insider and outsider, on how I should work with people who have been criminalized, as well as what ethical issues, tensions, and consequences I would encounter. For my research, I mobilized a critical ethnographic approach, or a *criminology of the criminalized*, one focused from the perspectives of criminalized people. This approach is grounded in critical social science, which promotes an ethics of taking a political stance in one's work, and in institutional ethnography, which asks questions from the perspective of those at the disjuncture of experience and institutional framings. To counter dominant institutional understandings of people living with HIV, I wanted to develop knowledge that came from the actual experiences and perspectives of criminalized people. I sought to conduct research to help to counter the logic of constructing people into cases, to oppose the violence enacted by police, public health authorities, the media, prisons, jails, and courts. But, in turn, have I not done the same thing to those who I have studied? How am I implicated in the production of cases? To elaborate this further, I'll share a final experience from one of people I interviewed, who I refer to with the pseudonym Stephanie. Part of her story was mentioned when I gave my testimony to the House of Commons.

STEPHANIE

I went to visit Stephanie in 2018. She had been criminally prosecuted on charges of aggravated sexual assault for allegedly not disclosing her HIV-positive status to several sexual partners. She had a hard time talking about what had happened to her. She had been sexually assaulted at a party by multiple men while she was blacked out on booze. The next day, she went to the police to tell them what happened. In the end, the police told her that she was the one being charged with aggravated sexual assault because she had not disclosed her HIV-positive status to them—in the context of her own gang rape. As someone who had been engaged in sex work for years, she was somewhat known to police, and her experience of assault was not considered valid. It was hard not to get angry and dismayed when hearing Stephanie's experience; it was such a perverse and twisted outcome of the criminal legal system, but not an uncommon one.

Stephanie had been just released six weeks prior from prison after spending multiple years inside. She had pled guilty because she had an inexperienced lawyer and feared the charge. If she pled, she could get a lesser sentence and could go be with her family.

Stephanie was in her late forties and when I met her she was mandated to stay in transitional housing under strict conditions, including a curfew. We spent a few days together talking about her life and experiences. She showed me around her transitional housing unit, and we went to some appointments together, walked around the city, hung out with her boyfriend, and shared some meals. She told me about her legal case, the challenges of probation and living under constant surveillance, and what it felt like to have her privacy and autonomy taken away.

Her story had been widely sensationalized in the media, with terrible headlines vilifying her as a violent perpetrator, headlines that were completely out of sync with her own experiences and reality. HIV was not transmitted in any of the instances. Headlines that now haunt her everywhere she goes, as those stories are forever indexed and searchable online.

Stephanie was a funny, kind, and generous woman who had been abused, sexually assaulted, and exploited by numerous men in her life. She understood herself as a good person who was being victimized by a broken legal system. Like others I met, she had been silenced, incapacitated, and had her freedom taken away. Her story was taken from her, now told by the police, Crown prosecutors, and journalists in the media.

Interestingly, the neighborhood that Stephanie was mandated to live in was close in proximity to where another researcher had been doing research into Stephanie's life. A few years prior to my visit, the researcher, who works in a major Canadian university had published research on Stephanie's case. In the publication, the researcher examined details about Stephanie's life—which had previously been published by the media and in court documents. In the academic text, the researcher analyzed Stephanie's experiences in relation to academic concepts and came to conclusions that might be understood to help advance knowledge on those concepts. The academic was sympathetic to Stephanie's case and was employing a critical analysis of the criminal legal system and of HIV criminalization.

I asked Stephanie if she knew there was academic literature written about her and that the researcher who had studied her worked not far from her where we were. Stephanie was shocked and said she had no idea. I showed her the text, with her full name, HIV status, criminal charges, and intimate details about her case (as was understood by institutions) printed across the page. Not only had Stephanie already lost all sense of privacy and decision-making about her life, but now she had become an academic case to be studied and analyzed without her knowledge by this other researcher. While the researcher was claiming to be in support of Stephanie and the argument was slanted against her being criminalized, the researcher published her life details without her consent, distributed as a knowledge commodity for the benefit of academia.

The practice that this researcher used is commonplace among those who study law and crime—even if they are critical of practices of criminalization. It has become understood as natural that people who have been alleged to commit crimes lose agency over the telling of their stories. It is considered a legitimate practice to turn people's experiences into cases to be studied.

As a qualitative researcher who speaks with people directly, interviewing them about intimate details of their lives, I am ethically obligated to garner consent to have them participate in my research. The process is rigorous and centered on an affirmative notion of consent, meaning the person can withdraw at any time up until the project has been published. Talking with people about their lives directly brings a sense of social and ethical accountability to the process. People shared with me because they want their experiences taken forward to amplify their voices in efforts to address the need for social change to undo the harms of criminalizing HIV. The research process becomes a reciprocal exchange and relationship aimed to support the community being researched and the researcher to undertake the project.

This other researcher did not officially require Stephanie's consent. The researcher only read about Stephanie using legal and media documents. Legal research and criminology often work with media and legal documents to construct actual people into cases to be studied. The epistemological trick of turning people into cases to be studied is a central part of doing research, and it is something I have done in this book.

Due to being criminalized, details about Stephanie's life are widely available online. A researcher could claim it is in the public interest and that it is their right since the person's experiences are now in the public domain. Some could argue that it is the public's right to know details about people who are charged and prosecuted with serious crimes and that there should be open discussion and analysis on their behaviors. But it is not a given that just because a person's life has entered the public realm that they can become fodder for academic inquiry. If a living person has entered the public realm due to being criminalized, and criminalized under laws that many deem discriminatory and violent, is it ethical to undertake research on that person without their knowledge or consent? Is it ethical to publish their name, personal health information, and criminal charges repeatedly? What of the right to be forgotten? Does the answer to any of these questions depend on a researcher's intentions? Perhaps not.

If a researcher aims to challenge the oppression of criminalizing processes with their work, what considerations should be taken about the kinds of sources that are used as data? Some forms of data (e.g., stigmatizing media articles and court prosecution and sentencing documents) have contributed to the oppression of the communities that the researcher is aiming to support. Had the police, media, and courts not breached Stephanie's privacy and produced a range of public information constructing her as a violent threat to the public, the researcher would have no source material as data. And indeed, I would never have known who Stephanie was and reached out to her.

Media reports come to be complicit in stigmatizing those labeled criminals, resulting in a range of forms of discrimination and violence against people. Every person I have met and interviewed for my research project who was in the media felt they were not fairly treated, and many think the narrative developed in court documents did not reflect what they understood to be true. Media articles had made it nearly impossible for Stephanie to get a job and support herself after incarceration due to how publicly she was known—policing and court files constructed her as sexual predator when she was the one assaulted.

Court documents are produced to develop a legal narrative of what took place in a specific instance. They aim to flatten complexity and nuance to conform to a binary logic of innocence versus guilt. They are "true" in as much as they aim to produce a legal outcome, the results of which are legal violence.

Working solely with documents created in the service of someone's criminalization, such as court documents, media articles, or police press releases or files, may only provide one account of experiences. Policing and legal documents that comprised her case were used to facilitate the incarceration of Stephanie. But her sexual assault was not on any official record, as it has been institutionally disavowed. There was no official public documentation of Stephanie's side of the story. So, what is missed when relying only on court and media documents as sources of data? Clearly in Stephanie's case, quite a lot.

I am not arguing that policing and court documents and media articles are not rich data sources or that they should not be used for research. Aspects of this book rely heavily on media, policing, and court research. But there may be implications for relying solely on those sorts of documents as primary sources when those same documents have been used to construct people as cases under criminalization, and when those same documents are used to justify legal and extralegal violence in the lives of criminalized people.

Could a researcher who focuses on telling criminalized people's stories risk unintentionally reinforcing the violence of their sources by relying on them as forms of truth? What is lost when experiences are turned into a "case" through criminalization, in academia, or otherwise? Why not choose to resist that form of reduction and abstraction and instead speak with people directly about their own experiences (when possible)? However, the outcomes of interviews will still be transformed into a case to be examined, as they have been in this book.

When I met Stephanie, after stopping at Tim Hortons, we sat in a park with coffee and sandwiches. In the distance, through the trees, we could see the university that the other researcher worked at. Stephanie was still shocked. It had not been difficult for me to get in touch with her. Stephanie was an actual person in the world who wanted to tell her story, to be heard and understood. I wondered if the researcher had ever thought it a possibility that Stephanie was a living person who might one day be sitting in a park near their university reading what was written about her.

I must be clear: I too am complicit in mobilizing Stephanie's case to make a point. But is my approach any different from that other researcher? I am not sure. I have been grappling with this question to help reformulate an ethical criminological analysis that originates from the social worlds of those who are criminalized, one that does not perform the same practices that the other researcher exercised on Stephanie. I should also state clearly that I respect this other researcher very much. But since this experience with Stephanie, and seeing the negative impact on her, I have been working to consider better ways forward.

One starting point as a way forward is to consider that other people are real, and that research with transformative aims must be situated in the communities it aims to support. Speaking directly with criminalized people helps to undo this epistemological disconnect and presents a counter narrative. Being able to elaborate what people know and how they come to be institutionally known, through understanding the actual experiences of criminalized people, is one way to make accountable harmful processes of criminalization and to undo the harms of developing knowledge that only reinforces those ways of knowing.

To support a criminology of the criminalized, I propose a series of questions that researchers wishing to work on issues related to criminalized people can ask themselves before approaching the subject:

What is my stake in this research?

How is my research question connected to the actual needs of criminalized people?

What are the lived experiences of criminalized people outside of how they are known and understood by institutions? If I am unsure, how can I find out?

What forms of violence do people face when being criminalized?

What are the origins/sources of that violence?

How are my sources of data implicated in that violence?

What actions in my work can I take to not reproduce that
  violence?
What actions in my work can I take to denaturalize that
  violence?
What are the institutional (or interinstitutional) narratives
  being told about criminalized people?
What disjuncture exists between the experiences of criminalized people and the institutional narratives?
How can my work provide a counternarrative to dominant
  institutional (or interinstitutional) ways of knowing
  criminalized people?
What would the person I am writing about think of what I
  am writing? If I am unsure, how can I find out?

This criminology of the criminalized, as a form of critical activist ethnography, can assist with putting into question the practices of mainstream forms of sociolegal and
criminology inquiry. Without being overly didactic, a criminology of the criminalized seeks to contribute to reclaim-
ing how the stories of criminalized people are told. Such an
approach has the potential to not enact forms of epistemological violence in the name of academic inquiry.

Such research can also look to the past to help understand
forms of criminalization in the present. Looking to the past
is one tool that critical researchers can mobilize in studying
forms of criminalization—from the perspective of the criminalized—to help analytically interrogate the present. The
process of looking to the past is part of working to denaturalize the violence of criminalization and to help hold systems and institutions accountable. Such an analysis does
not allow contemporary processes of criminalization to be
understood as a backfiring of the criminal legal system but
rather as something that was constituted over time through

deliberate actions and practices. Therefore, a criminology of the criminalized can also ask:

What historical practices shaped contemporary forms of criminalization?
How were criminalized people impacted under past regimes of criminalization?
What historical documents or records can be examined that elaborate the process of criminalization from the perspective of the criminalized?

Historical analysis like this can help ground critical research to ensure that forms of criminalization not be understood as natural occurrences or as matters of fate, but rather as social processes that need not be as they are, and hence are subject to change. Examining past forms of criminalization can help the critical researcher elaborate how certain types of people come to be labeled as criminals at certain moments in time due to a range of institutional forces. This form of analysis is one that rests on the assumption that society is always open to change—as it has been over history—and seeks to move toward a realm of human existence that is free from oppressive forms of avoidable violence and suffering.

The work of the critical ethnographic researcher aiming to counter the violence and suffering of criminalization is to call attention to the disjuncture between how criminalized people know the world around them, and how they come to be constructed into cases by criminalizing institutions. Working from the specific standpoint of people criminalized, the focus must be on the material consequences of being institutionally marked as a "criminal" and a "risk to public safety"—and the forms of suffering and violence that result. This approach disarticulates the person from their institutionally labeled *crime* narrative of innocence, guilt, repentance, and redemption. Instead, it examines the daily lives of people and how they come to be labeled as criminals and risks at certain points in time.

The primary orientation of this approach is toward the material impacts of criminalization, not the conceptual tools of the academy. With such an approach, documenting the ways in which the violence of criminalization operates is not done solely for the sake of documenting. An objective to contribute toward the advancement of academic thought is legitimate and vital. However, where social research could be urgently mobilized to advance material well-being and change the social conditions under which criminalized people live their lives, then the imperative of criminology of the criminalized must be in the service of criminalized people's needs first. Such an imperative moves research beyond mere description and objectification. Rather, research from the perspective of the criminalized can seek to contribute to critiques challenging the administration of punishment in society and to bear witness in support of calls for change. Perhaps most of all, criminology of the criminalized seeks to develop knowledge to support the political basis of a life worth living—one of flourishing—for people who have been subject to any form of criminalization.

Beyond Personhood

If the liberal conception of personhood enables the opposite, and personhood is the vessel through which violence is mobilized under criminalization, what is to be done? Roberto Esposito talks about how, in defining the human rights of certain subjects, rights language continually constitutes nonrights. As I mentioned previously, Esposito says, "the person not only includes its own proper negative within it, but constantly reproduces the negative."[1] Inherent in the notion of a person is the nonperson when a subject becomes less of a person, and their access to self-determination and autonomy are taken away. The suspension of rights to personhood for the risky, guilty, and criminal is justified as upholding the rights and protections of the so-called innocent and victimized. The citizen, then, has access to civil life as a protected person, while the noncitizen lives in precarity. Esposito presents this as an unresolvable conflict and an inherent problem within liberalism. Some may say the way out of this dilemma is via positive laws that protect human rights and equality. But within this thinking, the possibility of personhood being negated is still present.

The person as we know it is composed partially of legal instruments and processes that enable the realization of individualized liberal subjectivity. Throughout this book, we have read how the process of criminalization is one of violence that negates the personhood of the criminalized. Liberal notions of personhood are founded on the ability to negate the rights of persons for those regarded as morally unworthy. In a context of criminalization, unfounded fears of infection from HIV-negative people are privileged over the safety and well-being of those of us living with the virus.

In such a regime, once someone's legal personhood is deconstituted, the criminalized are no longer understood as worthy of protection, safety, or agency. People lost access to participating in public life. When they needed help, they were not heard. They lost access to autonomy, subjectivity, and the potential to flourish. For many, attaining legal personhood was already tenuous, since it is highly contingent on race, class, sexuality, and gender. On top of this, due to fears of the virus, people living with HIV, especially those who are racialized, gay, queer, and poor regularly live in a liminal space in the shadow of legal personhood.

In a Canadian settler context, the very notion of personhood for wealthy white settler women rests on the criminalization of Lizzie Cyr, an Indigenous woman and a sex worker who was living with a sexually transmitted infection. Cyr's punishment enabled the realization of certain forms of legal personhood for elite settlers. We live in a society that rests its foundation on violent forms of legal punishment. Seeking to redress the violence faced by negative persons may mean calling into question the liberal notion of personhood altogether.

What if notions of personhood in Canadian society, as well as other societies founded on liberal principles of individualism, private property, and free will, were not to rest on punishment and sanctioned violence? What if sanctioned and legitimate violence can be seen for what it is—violence?

While some forms of violence will always be inevitable, responding to violence merely with more violence is not a remedy; rather, this response will beget more violence and degradation. And if violence that is legally justified results in so much extralegal violence, how can the two be understood as distinct from one another? If violence begets violence, legal or extralegal, then the way out of this cycle is a social transformation towards a society that eschews reliance on violence altogether.

Healing can come when avoidable violence and suffering end. There is a way forward beyond legal violence. Such a social transformation can be realized through expansive understandings of protection and safety, which do not rely on punishment as a remedy. We can conceptualize a form of holistic personhood that does not rely on denying the humanity of one for the protection of the other.

There has been so much imagination and thinking beyond shallow solutions founded on the limits of violence. Abolitionist poet El Jones notes that a politics of transformation away from violence must come from ongoing relations of care between people, especially those most impacted by criminalization. [2] Queer author Zena Sharman outlines how communities of care mobilizing outside of institutions of violence will lead to health and well-being realized through collective organizing.[3] For both Jones and Sharman, a world beyond avoidable suffering is possible. To be fully realized, movements seeking to undo criminalization must have a long-term vision toward the abolition of legal violence. Such a vision must be grounded in racial justice and in the undoing of colonization. Remembering the past, like the story of Lizzie Cyr, is a reminder that HIV criminalization is not some sort of blip, anomaly, or backfiring of the workings of the criminal legal system. A system founded on racial and gendered violence will not stop producing violence until that system is undone.

The violence of criminalization is dependent on the liberal invention of individual personhood. Doing away with the harm and violence of criminalization will require moving toward notions of rights and autonomy that do not rest on existing nation-state legal and social structures that privilege individualist notions of freedom. This is an argument that asks us to look beyond existing mechanisms for redress and accountability. It will be the undoing of a system, which enables certain liberal legal protections for a few, to a new way forward that will result in greater protection for all.

Where Do We Go Now?

While the surveillance and violence of criminalization is all encompassing for those faced with it, there has been hope. In all the experiences of violence, discrimination, and suffering, criminalized people enact ongoing resistance in their daily lives. They have lived dynamic and rich lives, despite how they have been socially discarded and denied the rights of persons. Everyday acts of looking for employment, gaining self-confidence, and conceiving of a future slowly chip away at the confines of being denied the realization of personhood. All the people with whom I spoke for this book remain passionate, kind, funny, charming, and dynamic. They are people with visions for the future and individuals who wanted to share their stories for this project as an act of healing to seek justice and to turn what happened to them into a positive force for change. All the people were working to move away from the past in their own ways and are working on living their lives. At the end of my meetings with people, I asked them where they wanted to go, what they wanted to do, and what they wanted to be. For those I was still connected with, I also received updates on a regular basis.

STEPHANIE

Stephanie has been successfully fighting her case in court on appeal. She no longer lives in the transition house, and she lives a relaxed and happy life with her family in the country.

CYNTHIA

Cynthia told me that she was resisting the surveillance of police and her past client's stalking. She had a circle of friends, all sex workers, and trans women like herself. They created a scheduled communication and support network to surround Cynthia where someone was always on-call. When she needed to go out, one or more of the circle would join her, supporting her in the street to get groceries and go to appointments. "It is like a sisterhood, they watch out for me and protect me," she said. After more than a year, the charge of aggravated assault hanging over her head was eventually dropped by the Crown prosecutor.

JACKSON

Jackson is still incarcerated. He is often held in segregation, meaning he is alone for 23.5 hours a day in his cell. He regularly calls various organizations on the outside who provide support for him. In 2023, after a long appeal process, Jackson's first-degree murder charges were overturned, and a court lowered the charges to manslaughter. He is still designated as a dangerous offender.

ANGIE

Outside of what was shared in the media and in court documents, I do not know anything else about Angie. Much of her story is unknown to the public, and that is likely for the best.

SHAUN

Last time I spoke with him, he told me, "In the future I want to go to school, to college, I think I want to be a mechanical engineer because I have always liked mechanical machines and vehicles." He recently moved to a new city and said he no longer wants to think about the past. He had been working in a bar and was spending time with his dog.

FIG. 6.1. Where are people today?

LENORE

Lenore lost her appeal. She was sent back to prison. She gave birth in prison with guards watching over her. She was released back to her loving boyfriend and lives with him and their child. Last time I spoke with Lenore recently, she had been trying to save money so she could go to hairstylist school. She wants to move on with her life and hopes a job will help her stop relying on social assistance to survive. It was a challenge to get an interview for anything while being registered as a sex offender. Through a training and reentry program, she finally got a job. It took her a long time, but she was persistent. She said,

> I just got a new job today or yesterday working at a fast-food place. I'm trying to get off income assistance, and I'm really trying hard to get into a hairdressing course, that's my passion. I don't want to be on income assistance. Maybe once I get into that, I can eventually have a car and maybe rent or own a condo down the line or something.
>
> Despite everything, overall my family was really supportive and I am really resourceful. I did beat myself up a bit, I was on a destructive path right. But then I got to thinking, you know, I could let this disease and these charges kill me or I can rise above it and live the best life if I can, and that's the path I chose.

MATTEO

I had been in touch with Matteo off and on. Matteo had been going to school. He was in limbo jobwise since being released. He felt lost and now was facing jail time for this apparent violation. He had a long period of being depressed, was regularly denied employment, and was turned down by men while trying to date. But things had recently started to change. He told me, "I served my time, things have been hard. I'm just getting my life started again, relationship-wise, school-wise, I'm just starting to get a network of friends back. I have always enjoyed working for myself now, it's been finally going well."

He had been back to the village enjoying life, spending time with friends. But then I got that message on Facebook. Despite wanting to move on, the Sex Offender Registry was holding him back, and he felt he was under constant surveillance. He had served his time, but the registry was for life.

Whatever happened in the future with legal reform, or any sense of progress made by the Coalition did not mean much while people like Matteo were still in limbo, unable to realize a life of flourishing, a life of protection, of safety, and of autonomy over one's own future. I looked out my window at the night sky, the streetlights had just come on. Matteo had a warrant out for his arrest due to a minor violation of his sex offender conditions. He could go back to jail, a place that was the source of all his pain and trauma. I got on the phone and called a few people from the Coalition. Together we tried to get Matteo a lawyer to help him out. He has a pending notice to appear in court.

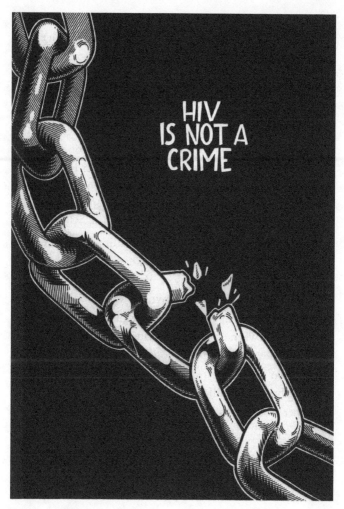

FIG. 6.2. HIV is not a crime

Notes

Foreword

1. K. Boulton, *Introducing the Sourcebook on U.S. State and Federal HIV Criminal Law: Pathways to Reform and State Perspectives on Building a Strategy* [webinar] (New York: Center for HIV Law and Policy, 2017), https://www.youtube.com/watch?v=_9hCuqjlYuU.

2. Center for HIV Law and Policy, *HIV Criminalization in the United States* [map] (updated 2022), https://www.hivlawandpolicy.org/resources/map-hiv-criminalization-united-states-chlp-updated-2.

3. Center for HIV Law and Policy, *HIV Criminalization in the United States: A Sourcebook on State and Federal HIV Criminal Law and Practice* (New York: Center for HIV Law and Policy, 2022), https://www.hivlawandpolicy.org/sites/default/files/HIV%20Criminalization%20in%20the%20U.S.%20A%20Sourcebook%20on%20State%20Fed%20HIV%20Criminal%20Law%20and%20Practice%20022722.pdf.

4. U.S. Department of Health and Human Services Centers for Disease Control and Prevention, *HIV Prevention in the United States: Mobilizing to End the Epidemic*, 2021, https://www.cdc.gov/hiv/pdf/policies/cdc-hiv-prevention-bluebook.pdf.

5. U.S. People Living with HIV Caucus, *Demanding Better: An HIV Federal Policy Agenda by People Living with HIV*, 2020.

https://www.pwn-usa.org/wp-content/uploads/2021/07/Networks
-Policy-Agenda-FINAL.pdf.

6. N. Cisneros and B. Sears, *Enforcement of HIV Criminalization in
   Louisiana* (Los Angeles, The Williams Institute, 2022), https://
   williamsinstitute.law.ucla.edu/wp-content/uploads/HIV
   -Criminalization-LA-Sep-2022.pdf.

7. Report of the United Nations High Commissioner for Human
   Rights, *Human Rights and HIV/AIDS*, 2022, https://www.ohchr
   .org/en/documents/thematic-reports/ahrc5053-human-rights
   -and-hivaids-report-united-nations-high.

8. R. Potter and J. Rosky, "The Iron Fist in the Latex Glove: The
   Intersection of Public Health and Criminal Justice," *American
   Journal of Criminal Justice* 38 (2012): 276–288, https://doi.org/10
   .1007/s12103-012-9173-3.

9. The Sentencing Project, *Growth in Mass Incarceration*, https://
   www.sentencingproject.org/research/.

10. U.S. People Living with HIV Caucus, *Demanding Better: An
    HIV Federal Policy Agenda by People Living with HIV*, 2020,
    https://www.pwn-usa.org/wp-content/uploads/2021/07
    /Networks-Policy-Agenda-FINAL.pdf.

11. Racial Justice Framework Group, *A Declaration of Liberation:
    Building a Racially Just and Strategic Domestic HIV Movement*,
    2017, https://hivracialjustice.wixsite.com/framework.

12. Ibid.

13. The Consensus Statement, *Consensus Statement on HIV "Treat-
    ment as Prevention:" in Criminal Law Reform* [policy brief], 2017,
    https://www.hivtaspcrimlaw.org/the-consensus-statement.

Preface

1. See Public Prosecution Service of Canada Deskbook, "Directive
   of the Attorney General Issued under Section 10(2) of the
   Director of Public Prosecutions Act, 5.12 Prosecutions Involving

Non-Disclosure of HIV Status," December 8, 2018, https://www
.ppsc-sppc.gc.ca/eng/pub/fpsd-sfpg/fps-sfp/tpd/p5/ch12.html.

2. G. Kinsman, "AIDS Activism: Remembering, Resistance versus
Socially Organized Forgetting," in *Seeing Red: HIV/AIDS and
Public Policy in Canada*, ed. Hindmarch, Orsini, Gagnon,
311–333 (Toronto: University of Toronto Press).

Chapter 1   Bearing Witness to Violence

1. A. Juhasz and T. Kerr, *We Are Having this Conversation Now:
The Times of AIDS Cultural Production* (Durham, NC: Duke
University Press, 2022).

2. A. Symington, E. J. Bernard, *Advancing HIV Justice 4: Understanding Commonalities, Seizing Opportunities* (Amsterdam: HIV
Justice Network, 2022), https://www.hivjustice.net/publication
/advancing4/.

3. See I. Grant, "Rethinking Risk: The Relevance of Condoms and
Viral Load in HIV Nondisclosure Prosecutions," *McGill Law
Journal* 54 (2009): 389–404; I. Grant, "The Prosecution of
Non-Disclosure of HIV in Canada: Time to Rethink Cuerrier,"
McGill Journal of Law and Health 5, no. 1 (2011): 7–59.

4. See C. Galletly and S. Pinkerton, "Conflicting Messages: How
Criminal HIV Disclosure Laws Undermine Public Health
Efforts to Control the Spread of HIV," *AIDS and Behaviour* 10,
no. 5 (2006): 451–461; T. Hoppe, "Controlling Sex in the Name
of 'Public Health': Social Control and Michigan HIV Law,"
Social Problems 60 (2013): 27–49; E. Myhalovskiy, "The Problem
of 'Significant Risk': Exploring the Public Health Impact of
Criminalizing HIV Non-disclosure," *Social Science & Medicine*
73, no. 5 (2011): 668–675.

5. E. Mykhalovskiy, "The Public Health Implications of HIV
Criminalization: Past, Current, and Future Research Direc-
tions," *Critical Public Health* 25, no. 4 (2015): 373–385.

6. J. Csete, R. Elliott, and E. J. Bernard, "So Many Harms, So Little Benefit: A Global Review of the History and Harms of HIV Criminalisation," *The Lancet HIV* 10 (2023): e52–61.

7. See J. Kilty, "Dangerous Liaisons, a Tale of Two Cases: Constructing Women Accused of HIV/AIDS Nondisclosure as Threats to the (Inter)National Body Politic," in *Within the Confines Women and the Law in Canada* (Toronto: Canadian Scholars' Press, 2014), 271–292; J. Miller, "African Immigrant Damnation Syndrome: The Case of Charles Ssenyonga," *Sexuality Research & Social Policy* 2, no. 2 (2005): 31–50.

8. V. Namaste, "AIDS Histories Otherwise: The Case of Haitians in Montreal," in *AIDS & the Distribution of Crises*, ed. J. Cheng, A. Juhasz, and N. Shahani (Durham, NC: Duke University Press, 2020).

9. A. Juhasz and T. Kerr, *We Are Having this Conversation Now: The Times of AIDS Cultural Production* (Durham, NC: Duke University Press, 2022).

10. M. Cifor, *Viral Cultures: Activist Archiving in the Age of AIDS* (Minneapolis: University of Minnesota Press, 2022).

11. S. Schulman, *Let the Record Show: A Political History of ACT UP New York, 1987–1993* (New York: Farrar, Straus and Giroux, 2021).

12. J. Cheng, A. Juhasz, and N. Shahani, *AIDS & the Distribution of Crises* (Durham, NC: Duke University Press, 2020).

13. H. Arendt, *On Violence* (New York: Harcourt, 1970).

14. F. Fanon, *The Wretched of the Earth* (New York: Grove Press, 1963).

15. W. Benjamin, "Critique of Violence," in *Selected Writings: 1. 1913–1926*, ed. M. Bullock and M. Jennings, 236–252 (Cambridge, MA: The Belknap Press of Harvard University Press, 1996).

16. J. Galtung, "Violence, Peace, and Peace Research," *Journal of Peace Research* 6, no. 3 (1969): 167–191.

17. Ibid., 168.

18. C. Murdocca, "'There Is Something in That Water': Race, Nationalism, and Legal Violence," *Law & Social Inquiry* 35, no. 2 (2010): 369–402 at 395.

19. E. Stanley, *Atmospheres of Violence: Structuring Antagonism and the Trans/Queer Ungovernable* (Durham, NC: Duke University Press), 6.

20. D. Garland, "The Problem of the Body in Modern State Punishment," *Social Research*, 7, no. 3 (2011): 767–798.

21. A. Sayer, "Who's Afraid of Critical Social Science?" *Current Sociology* 57, no. 6 (2009): 767–786.

22. N. Rose and M. Valverde, "Governed by Law?" *Social and Legal Studies* 7, no. 4 (1998): 541–551 at 545.

23. S. Merry, "The Criminalization of Everyday Life," in *Everyday Practices and Trouble Cases*, ed. A. Sarat, 14–40 (Evanston, IL: Northwestern University Press, 1998).

24. R. Maynard, *Policing Black Lives: State Violence in Canada from Slavery to the Present* (Black Point, NS: Fernwood, 2017).

25. C. Dayan, *The Law Is a White Dog: How Legal Rituals Make and Unmake Persons* (Princeton, NJ: Princeton University Press, 2011).

26. G. Agamben, *Homo sacer: Sovereign Power and Bare Life* (Stanford, CA: Stanford University Press, 1995).

27. R. Esposito, "The *Dispositif* of the Person," *Law, Culture and the Humanities* 8, no. 1 (2012): 17–30 at 24.

28. L. M. Cacho, *Social Death: Racialized Rightlessness and the Criminalization of the Unprotected* (New York: New York University Press, 2012).

29. G. Rubin, "Thinking Sex: Notes for a Radical Theory of the Politics of Sexuality," in *Deviations: A Gayle Rubin Reader* (Durham, NC: Duke University Press, 2011).

30. J. Mogul, A. Ritchie, and K. Whitlock, *Queer (Injustice): The Criminalization of LGBT People in the United States* (Boston: Beacon Press, 2011).

31. See "Anti-69 against the Mythologies of the 1969 Criminal Code Reform," https://anti-69.ca/.

32. D. Halperin and T. Hoppe, *The War on Sex*. (Durham, NC: Duke University Press, 2017).

33. S. Thrasher, *The Viral Underclass: The Human Toll When Inequality and Disease Collide* (New York: Celadon, 2022).

34. R. W. Gilmore, "What Is to Be Done?" *American Quarterly* 63, no. 2 (2011): 245–265.

35. Cheng et al., *AIDS & the Distribution of Crises*. (Durham, NC: Duke University Press, 2020).

36. K. Chavez, *The Borders of AIDS: Race, Quarantine & Resistance* (Seattle: University of Washington Press, 2021).

37. C. Hastings, N. Massaquo, R. Elliot, E. Mykhalovskiy. *HIV Criminalization in Canada: Key Trends and Patterns (1989–2020)* (Toronto, ON: HIV Legal Network, 2020), https://www.hivlegalnetwork.ca/site/hiv-criminalization-in-canada-key-trends-and-patterns-1989-2020/?lang=en.

38. Ibid.

39. E. Mykhalovskiy, C. Hastings, C. Sanders, M. Hayman, L. Bisaillon, *"Callous, Cold and Deliberately Duplicitous": Racialization, Immigration and the Representation of HIV Criminalisation in Canadian Mainstream Newspapers* (Toronto: CIHR Centre for Social Research in HIV Prevention, 2016).

40. E. Manning, *Why We Must Go beyond Focusing on the 'Overrepresentation' of Racialized People in HIV Criminalization*, 2019, http://somatosphere.net/2019/why-we-must-go-beyond-focusing-on-the-overrepresentation-of-racialized-people-in-hiv-criminalization.html/.

41. A. Sanderson, F. Ranville, L. Gurney, B. Borden, S. Pooyak, K. Shannon, A. Krüsi, "Indigenous Women Voicing Experiences of HIV Stigma and Criminalization through Art," *International Journal of Indigenous Health* 16 (2021): 267–290.

42. C. Hastings, N. Massaquo, R. Elliot, E. Mykhalovskiy. *HIV Criminalization in Canada: Key Trends and Patterns (1989–2020)* (Toronto, ON: HIV Legal Network, 2020), https://www .hivlegalnetwork.ca/site/hiv-criminalization-in-canada-key -trends-and-patterns-1989-2020/?lang=en.

43. C. Hastings, N. Massaquo, R. Elliot, E. Mykhalovskiy. *HIV Criminalization in Canada: Key Trends and Patterns (1989–2020)* (Toronto, ON: HIV Legal Network, 2020), https://www .hivlegalnetwork.ca/site/hiv-criminalization-in-canada-key -trends-and-patterns-1989-2020/?lang=en.

44. H. Washington, *Carte Blanche: The Erosion of Medical Consent* (New York: Columbia Global Reports, 2021).

45. T. Hoppe, *Punishing Disease: HIV & the Criminalization of Sickness* (Oakland: University of California Press, 2018), 69.

46. G. Kinsman, "AIDS Activism: Remembering, Resistance versus Socially Organized Forgetting," in *Seeing Red: HIV/AIDS and Public Policy in Canada*, ed. Hindmarch, Orsini, Gagnon, 311–333 (Toronto: University of Toronto Press).

47. S. Stern, *The Trials of Nina McCall: Sex, Surveillance and the Decades-Long Government Plan to Imprison "Promiscuous" Women* (Boston: Beacon Press, 2018).

48. J. Cassel, *The Secret Plague: Venereal Disease in Canada, 1838–1939* (Toronto: University of Toronto Press, 1987).

49. T. Hoppe, *Punishing disease: HIV & the criminalization of sickness* (Oakland, CA: University of California Press, 2018).

50. Criminal Code, section 238.

51. Ibid.

52. D. Bright, "Loafers Are Not Going to Subsist upon Public Credulence: Vagrancy and the Law in Calgary, 1900–1914," *Labour/Le Travail* 36 (1995): 37–58 at 58.

53. S. Burton, *The Person behind the Persons Case*, March 8, 2017, https://www.canadashistory.ca/explore/women/the-person -behind-the-persons-case.

54. R. Sharpe and P. McMahon, *The Persons Case: The Origins and Legacy of the Fight for Legal Personhood* (Toronto: University of Toronto Press, 2007).

55. Burton, *The Person behind the Persons Case.*

56. E. Murphy, Letter to Gordon Bates [Personal Correspondence], Volume 45, File 1, Health League of Canada Fonds, Ottawa, ON, Canada: National Archives of Canada, January 8, 1920.

57. K. Stote, The coercive sterilization of Aboriginal women in Canada. *American Indian Culture and Research Journal*, 36(3), 117–150 (2012).

58. Burton, *The Person behind the Persons Case.*

59. D. Bright, "The Other Man: Lizzie Cyr and the Origins of the 'Persons Case,'" *Canadian Journal of Law and Society* 13, no. 2 (1998): 99–115 at 101.

60. See Alberta Provincial Department of Health, *Annual Report of the Director of the Division of Venereal Diseases.* Calgary, AB, Canada: Alberta Provincial Department of Health, (1921, December 31); and J. D. McGinnis, "From salvarsan to penicillin: Medical science and VD control in Canada," in J. D. McGinnis & W. Mitchinson (Eds.), *Essays in the history of Canadian medicine* (Toronto, ON, Canada: McClelland and Stewart), 126–147.

61. A. Sayer, *Method in Social Science: A Realist Approach* (New York: Routledge, 2009).

62. D. Smith, *Institutional Ethnography: A Sociology for People* (Walnut Creek, CA: AltaMira Press, 2005).

63. V. Namaste, T. Vukov, N. Saghie, R. Williamson, J. Valle, M. Lefraniére, M.J. Leroux, A. Monette, J.J. Gilles, *HIV Prevention and Bisexual Realities* (Toronto: University of Toronto Press, 2012).

64. b. hooks, *Talking Back: Thinking Feminist, Thinking Black* (New York: Routledge, 2015).

65. A. Simpson, *Mohawk Interruptus: Political Life across the Borders of Settler States* (Durham, NC: Duke University Press, 2014).

66. C. Watkins-Hayes, *Remaking a Life: How Women Living with HIV/AIDS Confront Inequality* (Berkeley: University of California Press, 2019).

67. S. Sontag, *Regarding the Pain of Others* (New York: Picador, 2003).

Chapter 2 The Making of a Case

1. G. Smith, "Talking Politics—Police Shape Politics of AIDS," 1987, https://aidsactivisthistory.omeka.net/items/show/627.

2. M. N. Mensah, *Ni vues ni connues? Femmes, VIH et medias* (Montréal: Les Éditions de remue-ménage, 2003), 125.

3. B. Wilhelm, "AIDS Spreader Gets Year," *Edmonton Journal*, August 11, 1989, A1.

4. "Man Charged with Spreading AIDS Virus Regrets Actions," *Saskatoon Star-Phoenix*, April 13, 1989.

5. See C. Bell and K. Schreiner, "The International Relations of Police Power in Settler Colonialism: The 'Civilizing' Mission of Canada's Mounties," *International Journal: Canada's Journal of Global Policy Analysis* 73, no. 1 (2018): 111–128; J. Monaghan, "Mounties in the Frontier: Circulations, Anxieties, and Myths of Settler Colonial Policing in Canada," *Journal of Canadian Studies* 47, no. 1 (2013): 122–148.

6. See F. Barré-Sinoussi, S.S. Abdool Karim, J. Albert, L.G. Bekker, C. Beyrer, P. Cahn, A. Calmy, B. Grinsztejn, A. Grulich, A. Kamarulzaman, N. Kumarasamy, M.R. Loutfy, K.M. El Filali, S. Mboup, P. Munderi, V. Pokrovsky, A.M. Vandamme, Y. Young, and P. Godfrey-Faussett, "Expert Consensus Statement on the Science of HIV in the Context of Criminal Law," *Journal of the International AIDS Society* 21, no. 7 (2018): 1–12.

7. "HIV Carrier's Sex Assault Charge Sparks A-G Review," *Vancouver Sun*, November 30, 1991, A4.

8. Ibid.

9. P. O'Neil, "Women's Groups Object to Charge," *Vancouver Sun*, December 12, 1991, 4.

10. See Statistics Canada, *Correctional Services Statistics*, https://www150.statcan.gc.ca/n1/pub/71-607-x/71-607-x2019018-eng.htm.

11. F. Fanon, *The Wretched of the Earth* (New York: Grove Press, 1963).

12. L. Beaman-Hall, "Legal Ethnography: Exploring the Gendered Nature of Legal Method," *Critical Criminology* 7, no. 1 (1996): 53–70 at 58.

13. Ibid., 58.

14. Ibid., 58.

15. Ibid., 62.

16. D. Smith, *The everyday world as problematic: A feminist sociology* (Boston, MA: Northeastern University Press, 1987).

17. See Statistics Canada, *Criminal Victimization in Canada*, 2019, https://www150.statcan.gc.ca/n1/pub/85-002-x/2021001/article/00014-eng.htm.

Chapter 3   Institutions and Information

1. J. Colebourn, "Hunt for Woman with HIV: Vanishes from Shelter as Sex-Assault Trial Nears," *The Province*, January 2, 1992, A1.

2. E. Mykhalovskiy, C. Hastings, C. Sanders, M. Hayman, L. Bisaillon, *"Callous, Cold and Deliberately Duplicitous": Racialization, Immigration and the Representation of HIV Criminalisation in Canadian Mainstream Newspapers* (Toronto: CIHR Centre for Social Research in HIV Prevention, 2016).

3. "Police Say [name removed] Failed to Disclose HIV before Sex, Charge Him with Aggravated Assault," *The Peterborough Examiner*, April 8, 2015.

4. D. Pritchard, "Man Murdered over HIV Status, Court Told," *Winnipeg Sun*, March 5, 2012.

5. D. Prichard, "New Trial in HIV-Positive Gay Lover Bludgeoning," *Winnipeg Sun*, July 7, 2014.

6. D. Smith, *Institutional Ethnography: A Sociology for People* (Walnut Creek, CA: AltaMira Press, 2005).

7. M. DeVault and L. McCoy, "Institutional Ethnography: Using Interviews to Investigate Ruling Relations," in *Handbook of Interview Research: Context and Method*, ed. J. Gubrium and J. Holstein, 751–776 (Thousand Oaks, CA: Sage, 2004).

8. C. Hastings, "Writing for Digital News About HIV Criminalization in Canada," *Canadian Review of Sociology/Revue canadienne de sociologie*, 59 (2022): 181–199.

9. S. Timmermans and J. Gabe, *Partners in Health, Partners in Crime: Exploring the Boundaries of Criminology and Sociology of Health and Illness* (Oxford: Blackwell, 2003).

10. C. Sanders, "Examining public health nurses' documentary practices: the impact of criminalizing HIV non-disclosure on inscription styles," *Critical Public Health*, 25, 4 (2015): 398–409.

11. S. Molldrem, "How to Build an HIV Out of Care Watch List: Remaking HIV Surveillance in the Era of Treatment as Prevention," *First Monday*, 25, 10 (2020).

12. Corrections Service Canada, *Corrections and Conditional Release Statistical Overview* (Ottawa: Corrections Service Canada, 2021).

13. See "Overrepresentation of Black People in the Canadian Criminal Justice System," https://www.justice.gc.ca/eng/rp-pr/jr/obpccjs-spnsjpc/index.html.

14. Ontario Superior Court of Justice (ONSC), *R. v. Aziga*, ONSC 4592 (2011), 30.

15. J. Callwood, *Without End: A Shocking Story of Women and AIDS* (Toronto, ON: Knopf Canada, 1995).

16. J. Miller, "African Immigrant Damnation Syndrome: The Case of Charles Ssenyonga," *Sexuality Research & Social Policy* 2, no. 2 (2005): 31–50.

17. Ibid.

18. Ibid., 43.

19. Ibid., 43.

20. P. Adamick, "Can't Convict Ghost' Ruling in AIDS Case," *Toronto Star*, August 4, 1993, A3.

21. Ibid.

22. Ibid.

Chapter 4   A Typology of Violence

1. See R. Johnson, E. Gilchrist, A. R. Beech, S. Weston, R. Takriti, and R. Freeman, "A Psychometric Typology of U.K. Domestic Violence Offenders," *Journal of Interpersonal Violence*, 21, no. 10 (2006): 1270–1285; J. R. Johnston and L. E. Campbell, "A Clinical Typology of Interparental Violence in Disputed-Custody Divorces," *American Journal of Orthopsychiatry*, 63, no. 2 (1993): 190–199.

2. See H. V. Hall and R. S. Ebert, *Violence Prediction: Guidelines for the Forensic Practitioner* (Springfield, IL: Charles C Thomas, 2002).

3. J. Galtung, "Violence, Peace, and Peace Research," *Journal of Peace Research* 6, no. 3 (1969): 167–191 at 177.

4. S. Clark, *Overrepresentation of Indigenous People in the Canadian Criminal Justice System: Causes and Responses,* Department of Justice Canada, 2019).

5. P. Farmer, "On Suffering and Structural Violence: A View from Below," *Daedalus* 125, no. 1 (1996): 261–283.

6. Ibid., 273.

7. A. Davis, *Women, Race & Class* (New York: Vintage Books, 1983).

8. Office of the Chief Coroner Ontario, *M. H. D. Inquest Report November 6 2008* [report] (Ontario: Province of Ontario, 2008).

9. M. Mandel, "HIV-Positive Man Pleads Guilty after Unprotected Sex," *Toronto Sun*, November 23, 2012.

10. Galtung, "Violence, Peace, and Peace Research," 168.

Chapter 5   Testimony

1. S. Krämer and S. Weigel, *Testimony/Bearing Witness Epistemology, Ethics, History and Culture* (New York: Roman & Littlefield International, 2017).

2. Agamben, G., *Remnants of Auschwitz: The Witness and the Archive* (New York: Zone Books, 2002).

3. Ibid.

4. R. Elliott, *Criminal Law and HIV/AIDS: Final Report* [report] (Montreal: Canadian HIV/AIDS Legal Network & Canadian AIDS Society, 1996).

5. A. Choudry, *Learning Activism: The Intellectual Life of Contemporary Social Movements* (Toronto: University of Toronto Press, 2015).

6. S. Epstein, *Impure Science AIDS, Activism, and the Politics of Knowledge* (Berkeley: University of California Press, 1998)

7. See Bringing Science to Justice, 2023, https://www.youtube.com/watch?v=yuzuXgA29CU.

8. E. Mykhalovskiy, "Making Science Count: Significant Risk, HIV Non-disclosure and Science-Based Criminal Law Reform: A Reflexive Analysis," in *Criminalising Contagion Legal and Ethical Challenges of Disease Transmission and the Criminal Law*, ed. C. Stanton and H. Quirk, 150–174 (Cambridge: Cambridge University Press, 2016).

9. S. Schulman, *Let the Record Show: A Political History of ACT UP New York, 1987–1993* (New York: Farrar, Straus and Giroux, 2021).

10. See https://libcom.org/library/against-beyond-labour-interview-john-holloway.

11. A. Silversides, *AIDS Activist: Michael Lynch and the Politics of Community* (Toronto: Between the Lines, 2003).

12. M. L. Robertson, "An Annotated Chronology of the History of AIDS in Toronto: The First Five Years, 1981–1986," *Canadian Bulletin of Medical History/Bulletin canadien d'histoire de la médecine*, 22, no. 2 (2005): 313–351.

13. A. Silversides, *AIDS Activist: Michael Lynch and the Politics of Community* (Toronto: Between the Lines, 2003).

14. A. Juhasz and T. Kerr, *We Are Having This Conversation Now: The Times of AIDS Cultural Production* (Durham, NC: Duke University Press, 2022).

15. Public Health Agency of Canada, *HIV and AIDS in Canada Surveillance Report to December 31, 2008* (Ottawa: Public Health Agency of Canada, 2008).

16. A. Finkelstein, *After Silence: A History of AIDS through Its Images* (Berkeley: University of California Press, 2020).

17. T. McCaskell, *Queer Progress: From Homophobia to Homonationalism* (Toronto, ON: Between the Lines, 2016).

18. C. Watkins-Hayes, *Remaking a Life: How Women Living with HIV/AIDS Confront Inequality* (Berkeley: University of California Press, 2019).

19. See https://howtohavesexinapolicestate.tumblr.com/.

20. S. Epstein, *Impure Science: AIDS, Activism, and the Politics of Knowledge* (Berkeley: University of California Press, 1998).

21. K. Chavez, *The Borders of AIDS: Race, Quarantine & Resistance* (Seattle: University of Washington Press, 2021).

22. See Department of Justice Canada, 2016, https://www.justice.gc.ca/eng/rp-pr/other-autre/hivnd-vihnd/p1.html.

23. H. Solomon, "Canada's privacy law applies to Google search, says judge in right to be forgotten case," IT World Canada, July 15, 2021).

24. D. Spade, *Normal Life: Administrative Violence, Critical Trans Politics, and the Limits of the Law* (Durham, NC: Duke University Press, 2011).

25. G. Rubin, "Thinking Sex: Notes for a Radical Theory of the Politics of Sexuality," in *Deviations: A Gayle Rubin Reader* (Durham, NC: Duke University Press, 2011).

26. M. Kaba, "Part VI: Accountability is Not Punishment: Transforming How We Deal with Harm and Punishment" (pp. 132–163), in *We Do This 'Til We Free Us* (New York: Haymarket Books, 2021).

27. M. Kaba, "Part VI: Accountability is Not Punishment: Transforming How We Deal with Harm and Punishment" (pp. 132–163), in *We Do This 'Til We Free Us* (New York: Haymarket Books, 2021).

28. D. Parkes. Starting with Life: Murder Sentencing and Feminist Prison Abolitionist Praxis, in Taylor & Struthers-Montfort, eds, *Building Abolition: Decarceration and Social Justice* (New York: Routledge, 2021).

29. R. W. Gilmore, "What Is to Be Done?" *American Quarterly* 63, no. 2 (2011): 245–265.

30. See: A.Y. Davis, *Are Prisons Obsolete?* (New York: Seven Stories Press, 2003); L. Ben-Moshe, C. Chapman, A. C. Carey (Eds), *Disability Incarcerated: Imprisonment and Disability in the United States and Canada* (New York: Palgrave Macmillan, 2014).

31. See W. de Haan, "Abolitionism and the Politics of 'Bad Conscience'," *The Howard Journal*, 26, 1, 15–32 (1987); and Prison Research Education Action, Instead of prisons: A handbook for abolitionists: Chapter 7: Restraint of the Few, 1976, https://www.prisonpolicy.org/scans/instead_of_prisons/chapter7.shtml.

32. D. Parkes, "Starting With Life: Murder Sentencing and Feminist Prison Abolitionist Praxis," in *Building Abolition: Decarceration and Social Justice*, eds. Taylor & Struthers-Montfort (New York: Routledge, 2021).

33. Macallair, D., "The Closing of the Massachusetts Reform Schools and the Legacy of Jerome Miller," *Juvenile Justice Information Exchange* (January 4, 2012), https://jjie.org/2012/01/04/closing-of-massachusetts-reform-schools-legacy-of-jerome-miller/.

34. See https://www.nytimes.com/2015/08/16/us/jerome-g-miller-who-reshaped-juvenile-justice-dies-at-83.html.

35. N. Carrier and J. Piché, "On (In)justice: Undisciplined Abolitionism in Canada," *Social Justice*, 45, no. 4 (2018): 35–56.

36. H. Walia, *Global Migration, Capitalism, and the Rise of Racist Nationalism* (Black Point, NS: Fernwood Publishing, 2021).

37. See https://www.hivcriminalization.ca/take-action-as-an-organization/.

38. For further testimony of others, see https://openparliament.ca/committees/justice/42-1/142/.

Chapter 6   Conclusion

1. R. Esposito, "The *Dispositif* of the Person," *Law, Culture and the Humanities* 8, no. 1 (2012): 17–30 at 24.

2. E. Jones, *Abolitionist Intimacies* (Black Point, NS: Fernwood Publishing, 2022).

3. Z. Sharman, *The Care We Dream of: Liberatory & Transformative Approaches to LBGTQ+ Health* (Vancouver, BC: Arsenal Pulp Press, 2021).

Index

attorney general, 38, 58, 170, 182, 186–190

autonomy: depersonalization and, 1–3, 19, 29, 62, 87, 231–233; incarceration, probation, and, 140, 221–222; legal protections and, 17, 126; public safety and, 12, 99, 101; research, activism, and, 48, 51, 239. *See also* liberalism; personhood

bail: conditions of, 77, 205, 215; denial reversed, 58; denied due to severity of charge, 89, 108–110, 112, 129, 140, 205–206, 217; denied concerning public safety, 69: hearing, 68–69

Beaman-Hall, Lori, 79–80

Berkowitz, Richard, 178

Betteridge, Glenn, 188

Black Lives Matter, 182

Black men: increased criminalization of, xxii, 23–24, 53, 119, 161–165; media sensationalism and, 93–94, 117–123; police violence towards, 66–69, 140; trope of hypersexualized, 93, 117, 121–122

Black United Leadership Initiative, xxiv–xxv

Black women: children apprehended from, 32; exclusion of, 139

Black, Indigenous, and racialized people: experimental testing on, 29; HIV epidemics and, 22–23; legal facts and, 83; legal personhood and, 17, 231–232

blood: assault charges and, 28; CD4 count, 162, 164; personhood and, 18; tests, 132–133, 164; viral load in (*see* viral load)

bodily fluids. *See* blood; spitting

borders. *See* deportation; racialized migrants; undocumented people

Bright, David, 35, 40–41

British Columbia, 31, 57–59

Brown v. Plata, 14

Brown, Glen, 122

Callen, Michael, 178

Callwood, June, 122

Canada Border Services Agency, 24

Canada Diseases Weekly Report, 174

Canadian Association of Sexual Assault Centres, 59

Canadian Broadcasting Corporation, 191

Canadian Coalition to Reform HIV Criminalization, 170–171, 183–209, 239

capitalism, 21

Carrier, Nicholas, 199

Casey House, 122

Centers for Disease and Control and Prevention, xxi

Chavez, Karma, 21

Choudry, Aziz, 171

Clarke, Chad, 171, 189

colonialism: increased criminalization and, 4, 118–119, 125, 195–196; Indigenous people and (*see* Indigenous people; Indigenous women); legacies and histories of, xxvii, 26, 33–43, 58, 77, 137–139, 213–214; logics of, 54, 148–151, 153, 197–198, 214; roots of violence in (*see* violence: colonial roots of)

communicable disease criminalization, 32–42

community care, 2–3, 5, 106–107, 145, 174–190, 233–239. *See also* activism; community organizations

media, 218; anti-Black racism in, 23, 93–94, 117–124; early reports of HIV criminalization in, 56–59; incarceration and, 52–53, 56; incomplete or missing reports by, 28, 133, 158, 190, 218; institutional collaboration and, 99–104; labeled as public threat in, 2–3, 92, 95–99, 114–116, 222, 225; leading to violence and threats, 109, 123, 156–158, 186–187, 190–191, 218, 225; police and (*see* police: press releases by; public safety warnings); violence of, 94, 123, 190–191, 218. *See also* social media

medical: doctors (*see* doctors); expertise, 1–2, 81, 102, 179; files, 76, 82, 92; system, 101, 118. *See also* public health; public health: workers and officials

medical management of HIV: access to, 24, 26, 118, 130, 136, 162–164, 201; as a chronic and long-term condition, xxv, 1–2, 187; mandatory, 31, 111, 215. *See also* blood: CD4 count; viral load

mental health. *See* anxiety and PTSD; depression; law: mental health; psychologists and psychiatrists

mental health law. *See* law: mental health

Mikiki, 181

military, xx

Miller, James, 121

Miller, Jerome, 196–197

Ministry of Justice, xxviii–xxix, 60, 170, 186–189, 209, 212

Mogul, Joey, 20

Moore, Dawn, 168–169

Mulroney, Brian, 174–175

Murdocca, Carmella, 13

Murphy, Emily, 35–42

Mykhalovskiy, Eric, 23, 93

Namaste, Viviane, 4–5

narratives of HIV criminalization: countering dominant, 4–9, 44, 93–94, 171–172, 176–177, 186–187, 220, 228–230; institutional vs personal, 3, 62, 85–90, 99–100, 112, 212, 220–230; whiteness of, 4–5, 24, 29, 117–122, 172–173. *See also* law: facts in; victim: perpetrator *vs.*

national constitutions, 18, 33

New Democratic Party, 59

newspapers. *See* media and *names of newspapers*

non-consensual sex, 204–205: criminal charges for people who experienced, 84–85, 89, 152, 177–178, 200, 221; HIV transmission and, 74, 77, 134; incarceration and, 135–136, 145–148

non-disclosure of HIV: activism and (*see* aggravated sexual assault charge: activism and); conditions of criminalization for, xix, xxvii–xxviii, 22–27, 80–81, 170–171, 189–190; early histories of criminalization for, 55–60; in intimate partnerships, 56–60, 74–75, 89, 95–99, 107–110, 117–122, 162, 186–187; race and gender in, 24, 117–123, 204–205

nostalgia, 5, 172–173

Office of the Privacy Commissioner of Canada, 190–191

Ontario, 68, 93, 102, 119–122, 162–164, 174, 180, 182, 188–189

Ontario Health Promotion and Protection Act, 30–31, 121

About the Contributors

ALEXANDER McCLELLAND (HE/HIM) is an activist and researcher who is based on Ottawa, Canada. He is a professor at the Institute of Criminology at Carleton University, where he examines issues of criminalization, surveillance, public health, and policing. He is a member of the Canadian Coalition to Reform HIV Criminalization.

ERIC KOSTIUK WILLIAMS (HE/HIM) is a Toronto-based cartoonist and illustrator whose work explores queer culture and urban upheaval. His comics have appeared in *Dazed & Confused*, *The Believer*, and *PEN American*. He is an Eisner and Lambda Literary nominee. In 2023, Eric released 2 A.M. Eternal, collecting a decade of nightlife posters.

ROBERT SUTTLE (HE/HIM) is a prominent leader in the global HIV movement based in Brooklyn, New York. He is the chair of the Elizabeth Taylor AIDS Foundation Council of Justice Leaders, co-founded the Sero Project, and has received numerous awards, including the AIDSWatch Positive Leadership Award and recognition as a 2021 POZ 100 Honoree.

Available titles in the Q+ Public series:

E. G. Crichton, *Matchmaking in the Archive: 19 Conversations with the Dead and 3 Encounters with Ghosts*

Shantel Gabrieal Buggs and Trevor Hoppe, eds., *Unsafe Words: Queering Consent in the #MeToo Era*

Andrew Spieldenner and Jeffrey Escoffier, eds., *A Pill for Promiscuity: Gay Sex in an Age of Pharmaceuticals*

Alexander McClelland and Eric Kostiuk Williams (illus.), *Criminalized Lives: HIV and Legal Violence*